THEORETICAL DEVELOPMENTS IN HISPANIC LINGUISTICS
Javier Gutiérrez-Rexach, Series Editor

The Afro-Bolivian Spanish Determiner Phrase

A Microparametric Account

Sandro Sessarego

THE OHIO STATE UNIVERSITY PRESS • COLUMBUS

Library of Congress Cataloging-in-Publication Data

Sessarego, Sandro.

   The Afro-Bolivian Spanish determiner phrase : a microparametric account / Sandro Sessarego.

   pages cm — (Theoretical developments in hispanic lin)

   Includes bibliographical references and index.

   ISBN 978-0-8142-1265-3 (hardback) — ISBN 978-0-8142-9369-0 (cd) — ISBN 978-0-8142-7321-0 (e-book)

   1. Spanish language—Dialects—Bolivia—Determiners. 2. Spanish language—Dialects—Bolivia—Grammar. 3. Spanish language—Dialects—Bolivia. 4. Spanish language—Bolivia—Foreign elements—African. 5. African languages—Influence on Spanish. 6. Blacks—Bolivia—Languages. 7. Blacks—Bolivia—History. 8. Sociolinguists—Bolivia. I. Title.

   PC4876.S45 2014

   467'.984—dc23

                    2014003586

Cover design by James A. Baumann
Text design by Juliet Williams
Type set in Adobe Minion Pro

9 8 7 6 5 4 3 2 1

To Javier, Terrell, and Don

Contents

List of Tables

List of Figures

Acknowledgments

This study would not have been possible without the support of several people. I owe my gratitude to all of them. I thank the professors at OSU who showed interest in my work. My gratitude goes to Terrell A. Morgan, Javier Gutiérrez-Rexach, Donald Winford, Fernando Martínez-Gil, Scott Schwenter, Rebeka Campos Astorkiza, John Grinstead, Lisa Voigt, Laura Podalsky, Charles Klopp, Janice Aski, Peter Culicover, Luciano Farina, Cynthia Clopper, Fernando Unzueta, Mary Rose, Kathryn Campbell-Kibler, Anton Ryttin, Félix Julca Guerrero, and Laura Wagner.

I am obviously also indebted to Professor John Lipski, from Pennsylvania State University, who has always been willing to share with me his data and insights concerning Afro-Bolivian Spanish, and Armin Schwegler, from the University of California, Irvine, who patiently reviewed previous versions of this book and provided me with detailed feedback.

I must also thank Lorenzo Sangiacomo, my tireless travel companion and great friend, who accompanied me during several Bolivian journeys. Without his help I would never have been able to collect the data on which the present work is based. I am also grateful to José Luis Delgado (Pulga) and Sara Busdiecker, who offered me accommodation during my time spent in Los Yungas, and all the inhabitants of Tocaña, Mururata, and Chijchipa, who kindly welcomed me into their communities and let me bother them with questions and interviews for years. In particular, I would like to acknowledge Manuel, Maclobia, Reyna, Maricruz, Juana, Desiderio, Raymunda, Diego, Daniel, Daiana, Meagerly, Fabricio, Persi, Marta, Saturnino, Angélica, José, Juan, Francisco, Johnson, Dainor, Rafael, Víctor, Wilmer, and Sandra.

Special thanks go to Jill Robbins and to all the members of the Department of Spanish and Portuguese at the University of Texas, Austin, who have been extremely friendly and supportive with me since our first meeting, back in January 2014.

I would like to thank the Ohio State University for having provided me with generous financial support toward the realization of this study during my years spent in Ohio. I was lucky to be awarded the Post-Prospectus Research Award, the International Affairs Research Grant, the Alumni Grants for Graduate Research and Scholarship (AGGRS) Fund, the Josaphat Kubayanda Graduate Student Scholarship, two Graduate Student International Travel Grants, the Dr. Gordon P. K. Chu Memorial Scholarship, two Graduate Research Small Grants, the Council of Graduate Students Award, the Ray Travel Award, and the Loann Crane Award. Moreover, I must thank the University of Wisconsin, Madison for the research support that I have received. In particular, I would like to thank the University for the Nave Faculty Publication Supplement, the Fall Competition Award, the High Merit Research Award, and the Graduate School and Provost Subvention. I am also indebted to the Latin American, Caribbean and Iberian Studies Program and to its wonderful staff (Francisco Scarano, Alberto Vargas, Angela Buongiorno, Sarah Ripp, and Darcy Little).

I wish to express my gratitude to Mark Pietralunga and to the whole Department of Modern Languages and Linguistics at Florida State University in Tallahassee for being such a great group of kind and friendly people. None of this would have been possible without the support of my family (Simona, Marina, Fabrizio, Gianna, and Marino), and some people who have been very close to me and supported me in unbelievable ways here in the United States and abroad: Sarli Mercado, Juan Egea, Kata Beilin, Severino Albuquerque, Pablo Ancos, Ivy Corfis, Glen Close, Ksenija Bilbija, Fernando Tejedo, Alicia Cerezo Paredes, David Hildner, Loredana Comparone, Aaron Tate, Bill Cudlipp, Marcelo Pellegrini, Kathryn Sanchez, Ellen Sapega, Victor Goldgel-Carballo, Verónica Egon, Anna Gemrich, Elena D'Onghia, Gaetano Fossi, Giusy Di Filippo, Cosma and Noa Dellisanti, Daniele Forlino, Aria Cabot, Grant Armstrong, Rajiv Rao, Diana Frantzen, Grace Bloodgood, Tammi Simpson, Kate Fanis, Lucy Ghastin, Sean Goodroad, Leah Stenjem, Aurélie Rakotondrafara, Nyanda Redwood, Luca

Sessarego, Edith Beltrán, David Korfhagen, Melvin Rivera González, Manuel Delicado Cantero, Patricia Andueza, Raúl Diego Rivera Hernández, Manuel Díaz Campos, Rafael Orozco, Mario Rodríguez Polo, Isabel Arranz, Patricia González, Ignacio Sanz-Valero, Olin Johanssen, Wendy Feliz, Ivano Fulgaro, Mariano Escobedo Ávila, Juliana De la Mora, Pilar Chamorro, Daniela Salcedo, Maria Mazzoli, Giovanni Cristina, Carlo e Paola Forte, Magda Davoli, Magda Amhed, Irene Muzio, Sara Rossini, Morena Lanieri, Claudio Ferrari, Guido Borghi, Sara Rossini, Carlos and Midori Pimentel, Yassir Shekaldin, Marta Tallone, Gianluca e Filippo Garrone, Alessio Bianchi, Maria Grazia Biasotti, Cristina Anleri, Chiara Risso, Daniela Nebbione, Christian Emilio, Pablo and Holly Chignoli, Giandomenico and Antongiulio Caliendo, Giulia Obino, Massimiliano Parisi, Simone Lolli, Arturo Busca, Eugenio Daviso, Roberto Berritta, Ilaria Tassi, Marco Petrini and Mariana Lacunza, Brijesh Shah, and Alyssa Von Reuter.

Last but not least, I would like to thank Malcolm Litchfield and the Ohio State University Press staff for helping with the publishing process. Thank you!

1

Introduction

1.1. General Introduction and Objectives of This Study

During the last decade, the study of syntactic microvariation has received increasing attention. The main goal of syntactic microvariation is testing syntactic hypotheses and possible correlations between syntactic variables across closely related languages (Barbiers & Cornips 2001; Cornips & Poletto 2005). In particular, recent syntactic dialect atlas projects have taken such a research path. Two examples of current European projects aimed at studying microvariation are the Northern Italian syntactic dialect atlas (ASIS) and the syntactic atlas of Dutch dialects (SAND) (see Barbiers & Cornips 2001).[1] So far, little attention has been paid to the study of microvariation across Spanish dialects, especially to microparametric syntax across Afro-Hispanic contact varieties. From a theoretical point of view, what is fascinating about these languages is their richness in constructions that would be considered ungrammatical in standard Spanish.

The majority of the dialects that emerged in Latin America at the time of slavery from the contact of African languages and Spanish are not 'radical

---

1. More information about the ASIS (Atlante Sintattico d'Italia) and SAND (Syntactic Atlas of the Dutch Dialects) projects can be found at http://asis-cnr.unipd.it and http://meertens.nl/projecten/sand/sandeng.html.

creoles,'[2] languages highly influenced by substrate patterns, which would be unintelligible for a standard Spanish (stSp) speaker; rather, these varieties often consist of comprehensible vernaculars with a comparatively reduced inflectional morphology, and with other clear traces of fossilized second language acquisition strategies. Besides, from a purely linguistic point of view, these dialects might be considered even more natural systems, as they contain constructions which survived leveling phenomena imposed elsewhere by standardization processes (Weiß 2001).

To indicate the nature of their situation, halfway between 'radical-creoles' and standard systems, the terms 'semi-creoles' (Holm 1992) and 'partially restructured languages' (Holm 2004) have been proposed in the literature on contact linguistics. Their close relatedness to the standard can provide linguists with a great empirically-based testing ground for formal hypotheses (see Kayne 1996, 2000).

This work has a twofold aim. The first objective is to provide a syntactic description of the Afro-Bolivian Spanish (ABS) Determiner Phrase (DP). This dialect presents phenomena that offer a real challenge to current linguistic theory. For this reason, the present investigation accurately explores ABS DP structures. This analysis provides a testing ground for current linguistic hypotheses, and when appropriate, it proposes new solutions in light of the collected empirical data. The second goal is to shed light on the origin of ABS by analyzing the available sociohistorical data as well as the linguistic evidence found in this language. Particularly, I will test whether a creole hypothesis (Lipski 2008) can be proposed for this language or a different explanation should be provided instead.

1.2. Theoretical Framework

The language architecture assumed in this study is the one provided by the Minimalist Program (Chomsky 1995, 2000, 2001). According to this research program, the language faculty, the module of the human mind devoted to language, is defined by a small number of syntactic operations (*Merge, Move, and Agree*). The cyclical application of *Merge* and *Move* builds constituent

---

2. In this book the expression 'radical creole' is mentioned on several occasions. In the literature on creolistics, this expression is often used to indicate that the language formed rapidly, within a generation, usually via nativization of a pidgin. Nevertheless, in the current work, I am employing it with the meaning of 'language remarkably divergent from the superstrate,' without necessarily referring to its stages of formation.

structure. The operation *Merge* selects two items from the collection of lexi-cal elements (Numeration) and combines them. The operation *Move* creates a copy of a certain element and merges it in a different part of the syntactic structure. The syntactic constituent must receive an overt form; this overt realization occurs at Spell-Out, where the derivation splits and results in two independent paths, leading to two separate representations: Logic Form (LF) and Phonetic Form (PF).

Agree, on the other hand, does not create constituent structure. The operation *Agree* is a formal mechanism for valuation of certain features (unvalued) and deletion of others (uninterpretable) in the narrow syntax. In fact, in the most recent formulations of the Minimalist Program (Chom-sky 2001, 2002), syntactic derivations are viewed as strictly dependent on feature valuation and checking. The distinction between interpretable and uninterpretable features has proven very useful. Several features have an interpretation at Logic Form (LF); thus they are semantically-interpretable features. Other features lack such semantic import and are present to trigger the necessary operations during the derivation. Said uninterpretable fea-tures have to be matched via *Agree* and are finally deleted before Spell-Out.

(1)

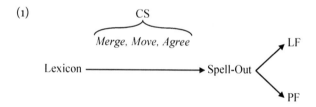

1.3. Organization of the Volume

Chapter 1 consists of a general overview of this work. It presents the current study's objectives as well as the theoretical framework assumed to analyze the data.

Chapter 2 provides a sociohistorical and linguistic account for the devel-opment of Afro-Bolivian Spanish to shed light on its origin.

Chapter 3 illustrates a variety of linguistic models that have been pro-posed to account for language variability. This chapter elaborates on the importance of enhancing a stronger dialogue between formal generative theory and sociolinguistic methodology, in line with recent microparamet-ric studies (Adger & Smith 2005; Barbiers & Cornips 2001). In doing this, chapter 3 provides a description of the methodology employed for data collection.

Chapter 4 offers a description of the most important issues concerning the generative study of the nominal domain during the last forty years. It begins with an account of the main assumptions behind the stipulation of the DP Hypothesis, and then illustrates several related studies that have contributed to the evolution of syntactic theories of DP. Chapter 4 provides an outline of frameworks and ideas that will be evaluated in this book according to the empirical data encountered for ABS.

Chapter 5 provides a detailed account of bare nouns in ABS. It tests Chierchia's (1998) Nominal Mapping Parameter and speculates on the nature of the ABS nominal domain in light of Longobardi's (1994) generalization on the structure of DPs.

Chapter 6 surveys N-ellipses in stSp and ABS. It analyzes the differences and similarities encountered in these two languages. Results will provide a testing ground for previous theoretical models developed exclusively on stSp data. Microparametric findings will also allow us to build novel generalizations to account for the cross-linguistic facts.

Chapter 7 focuses on processes of gender and number agreement across the ABS DP. The analysis assumes current minimalist models of feature valuation (Pesetsky & Torrego 2007), which partially contrast with previous assumptions on the nature of Agree (Chomsky 1995). Cross-dialectal differences between Afro-Bolivian Spanish and standard Spanish are accounted for in a systematic fashion, as computationally determined by differences in the specification of lexical and functional items and by restrictions on syntactic operations.

Chapter 8 analyzes variable number and gender agreement marking across the ABS DP. This chapter tries to enhance a long-awaited dialogue between quantitative sociolinguistic methodology and syntactic generative theory. In line with several sociolinguistic studies, this study recurs to a statistical software program (VARBRUL) to analyze cases of variable gender/number agreement. Nevertheless, differently from traditional sociolinguistic investigations, results are explained by adopting recent minimalist assumptions on agreement and feature valuation processes (Frampton & Gutmann 2000).

Finally, Chapter 9 summarizes the content of the present volume and provides the conclusions to this study.

A Sociohistorical and Linguistic Sketch of Afro-Bolivian Spanish

2.0. Introduction

Afro-Bolivian Spanish (ABS) is a dialect spoken in the region of Los Yungas, Department of La Paz, Bolivia. The first linguist to conduct extensive fieldwork on this language was John Lipski (2006a, b; 2008), who provided a thorough account of its grammatical features. Nevertheless, the exact origin of ABS is not yet completely clear. The present chapter will try to cast light on this issue. Lipski proposes that traditional ABS might have derived from an earlier pidgin and adds that "in the absence of any other viable scenario, *Afro-Yungueño Spanish must be viewed as the descendant of a colonial Afro-Hispanic pidgin* (2008: 186)." In fact, by looking at the "radically simplified VP and DP of the basilectal Afro-Yungueño dialect," Lipski (2006b: 37) hypothesizes a possible creole origin for this vernacular, which, after undergoing a process of decreolization due to contact, would now be in one of its final stages, closer to more prestigious regional Bolivian Spanish. Such a process would have taken place during the last fifty to sixty years, immediately after the Land Reform of 1952, which freed Afro-Bolivians from forced peonage. Nevertheless, the author recognizes the lack of reliable sociodemographic data; for this reason, he does not discard the hypothesis of "a stable but not creolized variety of Spanish that co-existed with Highland Bolivian Spanish since its inception" (Lipski 2006b: 37).

In this chapter, the available sociohistorical and linguistic evidence is examined. An alternative explanation will be explored to determine whether the grammatical elements reported by Lipski could be due to different phenomena, not necessarily linked to a previous Afro-Hispanic pidgin stage. In particular, the presence of these features in ABS is analyzed as the result of intermediate and advanced second language acquisition processes and only partial restructuring, which left room in this dialect for much of the morphosyntactic patterns encountered in Spanish. The development and crystallization of this contact variety took place in isolated rural communities, unaffected by standardization processes imposed by urban society and linguistic norms. The outcome is a vernacular, understandable by monolingual standard Spanish speakers, which carries the undeniable trace of second language learning strategies. The model proposed here for ABS not only considers the importance of social factors in patterning the presence of certain linguistic elements into this dialect; it also attempts to explain why certain constructions might have emerged as a function of universal processing constraints on learnability imposed by the human mind.

2.1. Terminological Clarifications

Even though the study of creole languages has grown substantially during the last few decades, it is important to remember that there is no consensus among linguists on what a 'creole language' is and on how the words 'creole' or 'creoleness' should be used. In fact, some scholars have tried to classify creoles according to their structural features (Bickerton 1981) or as a typological class (Seuren & Wekker 1986; McWhorter 1997, 1998, 2001; Bakker et al. 2011). Others have adopted a comparative structural approach that attempts to classify these vernaculars according to the relative distance from their lexifier languages, thus leading to more terms, such as 'semi-creoles' (Schneider 1990; Holm 1992) and 'intermediate creoles' (Winford 2000). Other linguists have instead suggested that 'creoleness' cannot be quantified (Muysken & Smith 2005), and therefore there are no linguistic parameters to define creole languages (DeGraff 2003, 2004). For this reason, some definitions prefer to depict these varieties as the by-product of their shared sociocultural history, often related to slavery (Mufwene 1997; DeGraff 2005), while others focus on their stages of development, suggesting that creoles are the result of a cross-generational break in language transmission (Thomason & Kaufman 1988), or indicating that these vernaculars should be seen as nativized pidgins (Romaine 1988). Finally, in a recent article on pidgin and creole studies, Schwegler (2010: 438) stated that it is the "combination of internal linguistic features and shared external history that gives creoles exceptional status." In his view, this is why "conceptual terminology such as 'creole', 'creolist', 'creolistic', 'creolization' and so forth continues to be applied without hesitation by most creolists, including those who reject the possibility of defining 'creole' as a class" (2010: 438).

Because of this wide range of definitions, I will have to put aside terminological debates and adopt for convenience Lipski's (2008) structural account. In fact, even though the author does not deny the importance of social, historical, and cultural factors in creating and shaping creole languages, he provides a feature-based account to determine where to place ABS with respect to other contact varieties and speculates on whether ABS might have developed from a colonial Afro-Hispanic pidgin.

As stated previously, I would like to propose a different hypothesis. In my view, ABS should be seen as the result of fossilized processes of second language acquisition, which crystallized in an environment removed from the pressure posed by the linguistic norm and language standardization. In order to back this claim, before providing the sociohistorical and linguistic evidence in support of my point, I will briefly introduce Processability Theory (Pienemann 1998, 2000, 2005), the Interlanguage Hypothesis (Plag 2008a, b; 2009a, b), and the theory of Vernacular Universals (Chambers 2003, 2004), three frameworks that will establish the theoretical basis on which to build the following discussion.

2.2. Processability Theory and the Interlanguage Hypothesis

Processability Theory (Pienemann 1998, 2000, 2005) is an SLA theory that attempts to account for the well-known fact that second language speakers acquire an L2 along a specific developmental path, in a systematic way. In order to explain why this is the case, the theory recurs to psycholinguistic models of speech production, as those designed by Levelt (1989) and Kempen & Hoenkamp (1987). Processability Theory rests squarely on the assumption that language processing procedures are activated according to a specific hierarchical sequence, which, in turn, drives their order of acquisition. Pienemann (2000) presents such a sequence by providing English data. In fact, research on English SLA has extensively shown that speakers tend

Table 2.1
Developmental Stages in English Interlanguage Syntax (Pienemann 2000)

Development	Structure	Example
Initial State	One-Word Utterance	*Ball*
	Canonical Word Order	*Bob kick ball (SVO)*
	Neg + V	*He no like coffee*
	Adverb Fronting	*Then Bob kick ball*
	Topicalization	*That I didn't like*
	Do-Fronting	*Do you like it?*
	Yes-No Inversion	*Has he seen you?*
	Copula Inversion	*Where is John?*
	Particle Verbs	*Take the hat off*
	Do/Aux 2nd	*Why did he sell that car?*
		Where has he gone?
Target	Cancel Inversion	*I wonder why he sold that car*

to universally follow the acquisition path reported in Table 2.1. They begin by pronouncing one word at a time; then they systematically develop more complex structures in a hierarchical order until reaching—in some cases—a target-like proficiency (see Plag 2008a: 123–124).

Recently, Plag (2008a, b; 2009a, b) has incorporated Processability Theory into his Interlanguage Hypothesis of creole formation. According to the Interlanguage Hypothesis, creoles should be seen as "conventionalized interlanguages of an early stage" (Plag 2008a: 115). Plag, in fact, tries to account for many aspects of creole grammar: loss of inflectional morphology, the supposedly unmarked nature of a variety of syntactic constructions, phonological simplifications, and several cases of word-formation, such as cases of circumlocutions, which are also typical of interlanguages. Our goal is not so broad. This study will be focused on providing an account for the features classified by Lipski as potential indicators of creolization. In the rest of this chapter, I will try to show that the "creole-like" features reported for ABS are not exclusive of an interlanguage of an early stage; rather, they are commonly encountered in intermediate and advanced interlanguages and sometimes also in non-standard Spanish and Portuguese dialects.

2.3. Vernacular Universals

A comprehensive account of the ABS creole-like features should not only be limited to the SLA/processing aspects of their development; for this reason, I will also provide a sociolinguistic framework able to explain why these features crystallized and survived in ABS in the way we know them today. A theoretical model, which I think can complement my hypothesis on the nature of these features, is the framework provided by Chambers' (2003, 2004) Vernacular Universals. In Chambers' view, a limited number of phonological and morphosyntactic phenomena seem to persist in vernacular varieties wherever they are spoken. Chambers (2003: 266–270) classified these recurring natural elements as "vernacular roots."

The theory of Vernacular Universals assumes that these vernacular features are in some sense more 'natural' than standard forms (see also Weiß 2001). Chambers takes a radical position on this issue and claims that they are the natural by-products of the language faculty, that is, the mental bio-program (or UG) that differentiates humans from other beings (Chambers 2004). I do not believe that these vernacular roots should be considered as the principles of UG. The way in which Chambers formulates his claim is reminiscent of Bickerton's (1981) Bioprogram Hypothesis, which has long since been proven to provide a misleading picture of pidgin and creole genesis. On the other hand, I believe that Chambers' observation that pidgins, creoles and second language varieties tend to share some common features that can be reinterpreted from a SLA perspective by simply saying that constructions requiring less processing are mastered before constructions requiring more processing, so that elements that are hard to process will not be encountered in the initial stages of these developing grammars.

Demonstrating naturalness for phonological processes appears to be easier than for syntactic ones. For example, consonant cluster reductions may be seen as the result of more economic motor-articulatory operations (Chambers 2003: 258–259). On the other hand, analyses that might account for more natural syntactic processes are more difficult to evaluate, and I think they could—and should—be questioned. For example, some doubts might be cast on whether Chamber's universal "double negation in English" is really more natural than single negation (see Chamber 2003: 129). It is true that it seems to appear in the majority of English vernaculars, but to claim that it represents a more natural form, some additional linguistic evidence should be provided: e.g., analyzing whether it is really easier to process or easier to acquire in an L2.

In the next section, I will present and analyze the "creole-like" elements found in ABS in order to determine whether they should be seen as traces of a previous stage of radical creolization or whether they could simply be ascribed to intermediate and advanced second language strategies that happened to fossilize in a language, which, until recently, was not affected by the standardization pressure imposed by society.

2.4. Afro-Bolivian Spanish Traditional Features

After extensive fieldwork in the Afro-Bolivian communities, Lipski was able to identify the most conservative features characterizing the traditional dialect. His work must not have been easy, on the grounds that, as he says, "full active competence [in the traditional vernacular] is probably limited to at most a few hundred [elderly] individuals, possibly even fewer" (2007: 178). In fact, as a consequence of the recent process of linguistic approximation to Spanish, many of the characteristic features of this language are partially or totally absent from the speech of the youngest generations. Table 2.2 presents some of the most traditional ABS features, those selected by Lipski (2008) as potentially salient for the creole hypothesis.[1]

In Table 2.3, Lipski compares the same Afro-Bolivian traditional features with those encountered in other Spanish/Portuguese 'creoles' (2008: 184), to determine the status of Yungueño Spanish with respect to them.

Lipski suggests that "at least impressionistically, Afro-Yungueño Spanish is more creole-like than the Helvécia (Brazilian) Portuguese dialect. At the same time, Afro-Yungueño Spanish seems less 'deep' than the creoles of Palenque (Colombia), São Tomé or the heavily substrate-influenced Chabacano varieties of Philippine Creole Spanish" (Lipski 2008: 183).

In the rest of this section, we will take a closer look at the features presented in Tables 2.2 and 2.3 to understand to what extent they may be taken as indicators of a previous creole stage. As I will try to show, these grammatical elements can often be found in advanced second languages and in substandard Spanish and Portuguese dialects, which did not derive from earlier creoles.

It is true that while null articles in subject position are not generally allowed in Romance languages (see Contreras 1986), they have been extensively

---

1. More recently, Pérez Inofuentes (2010) has also proposed a creole hypothesis to account for the origin of ABS.

Table 2.2

Examples of Afro-Bolivian Traditional Features, Salient for the Creole Hypothesis

Phenomenon	Example
Elimination of definite articles in subject position	Ø perro ta flojo [los perros están flojos] 'dogs are worthless'; Ø patrón huasquiaba Ø mujé [los patrones huasqueaban a las mujeres] 'the landowners beat the women'
Use of the Spanish third person singular as invariant verb form for all persons and numbers	Nojotro tiene [nosotros tenemos] jrutita 'we have fruit'; yo no conoció hacienda [yo no conocí hacienda] 'I never knew the haciendas'; yo miró jay [yo miré] 'I saw [it]'
Constructions based on invariant ta(ba) + infinitive instead of conjugated verbs	¿Quién ta comprá? [¿quién está comprando?] 'who is buying [coca]?'
Constructions based on invariant ya + infinitive instead of conjugated verbs	Furlano ya murí [murió] 'so and so just died'; Ya viní [vino] temprano tia Francisca 'Francisca came early'
Constructions based on invariant va + infinitive instead of conjugated verbs	Nojotro va trabajá [nosotros vamos a trabajar] 'We are going to work'; Yo va recogé mi lena [Yo Voy a recoger mi lena] 'I'm going to get my firewood';
Non-inverted questions	¿Cuánto hijo pue oté tiene? [¿cuántos hijos tiene usted?] 'How many children do you have?'; ¿ande pue oté viví? [¿dónde vive usted?] 'where do you live?'
Suspension of grammatical gender in nouns and adjectives	Tudu un [toda una] semana 'a whole week'; nuestro cultura antigo [nuestra cultura antigua] 'our traditional culture'
Use of nuay [Spanish no hay 'there is/ are not'] and nuabía [Spanish no había 'there was/were not'] instead of no tener 'to not have'	Yo nuay cajué [no tengo café] 'I don't have any coffee'; Ele nuay ningún marido nada [ella no tiene ningún marido] 'she does not have any husband at all'
Use of tener 'to have' instead of haber 'to exist' to express existence	Tiene un negrita qui taba aquí [había una mujer negra que estaba aquí] 'there was a black woman who lived here'; Tenía un señora, un negra '[había una señora, una negra] 'there was a woman, a black woman'
Occasionally, double negation with nada 'nothing'	Ningun misa nada [ninguna misa (para nada)] 'no mass at all'; Yo no va i nada [yo no voy a ir (para nada)] 'I am not going at all'

Table 2.3
Key Structural Features of Yungueño Spanish and Selected Creole Languages

	Yungueño	Helvécia	Palenquero	Papiamentu	Chabacano	Gulf of Guinea	Cape Verde
Null def. art.	Yes	Yes	Yes	Yes	No	Yes	Yes
Invariant verb form for person and number	Yes	Some	Yes	Yes	Yes	Yes	Yes
TMA particles	Maybe	No	Yes	Yes	Yes	Yes	Yes
Non-inverted questions	Yes	Yes	Yes	Yes	Yes	Yes	Yes
Pluralizing particle/3pl.	No	No	*Ma*	3 pl. (*nan*)	*Mga*	Some 3 pl.	No
No gender concord in NPs	Yes	Some	Yes	Yes	Yes	Yes	Yes
Subject pronouns as object	No (except *yo* after prep.)	Yes (except 1s.)	Yes (except 1s.)	Yes	No	Some	No
'to have' as existential verb	Some	Yes	Yes	Yes	Yes, in affirmative	Yes	Yes
Negation	Preposed (occasional double NEG with *nada*)	Double NEG	Postposed	Preposed	Preposed	Double NEG/ postposed	Preposed
NEG derived from no/não	Yes	Yes	Yes[a]	Yes	*Hendeq* and *no*	*Na . . . f(a)*	Yes
Postposed NP as possessive	No	No	Yes	No	No	Yes	No
Serial verbs	No	No	No	Some	No	Yes	Few
Predicate clefting	No	No	Yes	Yes	No	Yes	No

a. Schwegler points out that Palenquero negation system is actually more complex than what indicated in the table; it consists of NEG1 (preposed), NEG2 (embracing NEG), and NEG3 (postposed) (cf. Schwegler 1991).

reported in their derived creole varieties (e.g., on Cape Verdian, see Baptista 2007; on Palenquero, see Schwegler 2007). However, it must be said that they can also be found in Spanish and Portuguese dialects, which could hardly be classified as creoles, for example, in Chota Valley Spanish (Lipski 1992; Sessarego 2013) and Brazilian Portuguese (Guy 1981; Munn & Schmitt 2001; Schmitt & Munn 2003; Müller 2003).[2] Moreover, it is well known that second language speakers, coming from a first language with a different article system, or with no article system at all, can present bare nouns and article mismatches even at intermediate and advanced levels (Leonini 2006; Sánchez & Giménez 1998). Bickerton (1981) provides a description of how bare nouns should behave in prototypical creoles. In his view, these languages tend to present an article system with "a definite article for presupposed-specific NP; an indefinite article for asserted-specific NP; and zero for nonspecific NP" (1981: 56). Bickerton's analysis does not account for the features of Afro-Bolivian Spanish. In this dialect, in fact, there are three definite articles (*el, la, lu*), agreeing with the noun in gender and number, and two indefinite ones (*un, unos*), agreeing only in number. Their distribution is for the most part like the one of Spanish with the difference that bare nouns can take on either plural/singular, specific/non-specific/generic readings, given the proper pragmatic contexts (see Gutiérrez-Rexach & Sessarego 2011 for a detailed account). ABS bare nouns closely resemble Brazilian Portuguese ones (see Munn & Schmitt 2001; Müller 2003).

Verb forms showing invariable third person singular morphology are commonly encountered in L2 varieties (Slabakova 2009) and are often only mastered after intensive formal instruction. Since formal education has entered Los Yungas more recently (after 1952), it is not completely surprising to encounter the presence of these verb forms in the speech of the oldest Afro-Bolivian informants. Moreover, it is important to stress that ABS verb forms clearly inflect for tense and aspect (e.g., *tomó* 'he drank' and *tomaba* 'he was drinking'), while more radical creoles usually show invariant verb stems preceded by TMA (Tense, Mood, and Aspect) markers.

On the other hand, the grammatical particles identified as potential TMA elements for Afro-Bolivian Spanish seem to have been directly derived

---

2. Note that this is my personal opinion (see Sessarego 2013 for Chota Valley Spanish). In the literature, it has also been suggested that Brazilian Portuguese was a creole that decreolized. According to this view, bare plurals in this language would be the direct result of substrate influence (Guy 2004; Lipski 2006a). On the other hand, Naro & Scherre (2000) do not agree with this hypothesis and consider the differences between Brazilian Portuguese and Peninsular Portuguese as the result of 'normal'—internally motivated—language change (see Schwegler 2010 for an overview of this debate).

from Spanish where they are used in the same way. Moreover, Lipski recognizes that "Afro-Bolivian speakers effectively regard the use of *tá* + *verb* as a performance phenomenon, and indeed a comparison with the rest of the Afro-Yungueño corpus points to phonetic erosion [of the gerundive form] and unguarded speech as the origin of this construction. As such, it cannot be considered an integral part of the verb system of their dialect" (2008: 123). Furthermore, the analysis of *tá* as a creole preverbal marker should always be considered with caution. Unless we can document for ABS *tá* functions that are significantly divergent from Spanish *está* 'he/she is'—and this is not the case—the creole TMA status of this element should be questioned because of its close relation to /s/ weakening.

The analysis of *ya* as a TMA perfective marker is dubious too. Lipski (2008: 125) could report only a few instances, which closely resemble their Spanish counterparts:[3]

(2)   Fulano ya murí [murió]
      Fulano already die-INF [die 3-SG.PAST]
      'So and so just died'

(3)   Ya vení [vino] temprano tía Francisca
      Already come INF [come 3-SG.PAST] early aunt Francisca
      'Francisca came early'

The author indicates that these examples might consist of TMA markers followed by infinitive verb forms; nevertheless, given the similarities between these sentences and the Spanish ones and the lack of people's judgments on their grammaticality, we do not have enough evidence to classify them as TMA particles. Lispki himself casts some doubts on the possible use of *va* as future/irrealis marker (2008: 125–127). In fact, all Spanish dialects possess constructions of the kind *ir* 'go' + *a* 'to' + infinitive, where the preposition *a* may be absorbed phonetically by the third person singular form *va* (< *va a*). For this reason, the only difference between ABS and standard Spanish in this respect is the lack of person and number morphology on the verb form, which, as we saw, is a common feature of L2 varieties. Finally, Lipski also suggests that "there is no evidence that *tá, va* and *ya* once had particle status" (2008: 127).

_____

3. Schwegler (personal communication) points out that, in line with Palenquero, where 'a' acts as a TMA marker, examples (2) and (3) could actually be as follows: (2) Fulano *ya a murí* and (3) *Ya a vení temprano tía Francisca.*

Non-inverted questions, consisting of a fronted operator followed by a preverbal subject (*wh*-S-V), are not only found in creole languages; rather, they are also well attested in non-creolized Spanish dialects such as Cuban, Dominican, Puerto Rican, etc. (Lipski 1994). Furthermore, *wh*-S-V questions are found cross-linguistically also in very advanced L2s (Pienemann 1998, 2000), thus showing that they are not only indicative of creoles.

Full gender agreement operations are mastered late during the second language acquisition process (Bruhn de Garavito & White 2000; Franceschina 2005; Hawkins 1998; Leonini 2006); phi-feature agreement mismatches are quite common in L2s, especially if the learner speaks an L1 that lacks 'gender' as a feature (Franceschina 2002). Additionally, it should be pointed out that all ABS speakers, even the eldest members of the community, can clearly identify masculine and feminine nouns. Therefore, what differentiates ABS from standard Spanish is not the presence/absence of gender features, but rather the DP elements specified for agreement with the noun. In fact, while in Spanish adjectives, articles, demonstratives, and quantifiers all agree in gender with the noun, the operation Agree for this feature is just restricted to definite articles in Yungueño Spanish (Sessarego & Gutiérrez-Rexach 2011). The limitation of nominal gender agreement to these determiners inherently indicates the presence of the feature 'gender' in the dialect. In this respect, ABS is quite different from the majority of the Romance-based creoles, which are generally supposed to lack gender features.

The verbs *tener* 'to have' and non-auxiliary *haber* 'to exist' are usually respectively employed to express possession and existence; nonetheless, occasionally *nu hay* (Sp. *No hay* 'there is not') and *nu había* (< Sp. *No había* 'there was not') can be used to express lack of possession:

(4) Yo nu hay cajué
I no have coffee
'I do not have coffee'

The employment of *tener* as existential is only occasional, but may occur:

(5) En la mesa tiene gallina
in the table have chicken
'On the table there are some chickens'

Lipski proposes that the overlap between these two verbal forms may have

been greater in the past (2008: 181). This phenomenon may well be an indicator of partial restructuring; however, it does not imply any previous creole
stage.

Lipski (2008: 138) presents some instances of double negation with *nada*
and indicates that they are only occasional (6). Nevertheless, they should
not be taken as creole-like features since they are also encountered in other
Spanish and Portuguese dialects, which would hardly be labeled as creoles:
e.g., Brazilian Portuguese (Schwenter 2005), Puerto Rican and Venezuelan
Spanish (Lipski 2008: 138–139).

> (6) Oté no fue escuela nada
>   You no went school nothing
>   'You did not go to school at all'

In summary, only a few features of those indicated in Tables 2.1 and 2.2 as
indicators of previous creolization can be said to really belong to ABS. Such
elements are the following:

- Presence of bare nouns
- Use of the 3rd person singular verb form for all persons and
  numbers
- Non-inverted questions
- Gender agreement limited to definite articles
- Some overlap between '*tener*' and '*haber*'
- Some cases of double negation with '*nada*'

Moreover, we should stress that besides these elements, which are sugges-
tive but not necessarily evidence of the nativization of an early pidgin, the
majority of the morphosyntactic patterns encountered in ABS are also found
in Spanish. If we cannot obtain a precise picture of a language by ranking it
in terms of "creoleness," we can at least get a general idea of where it stands
with respect to other varieties. It is obvious that ABS is a contact variety
presenting several key differences from standard Spanish; however, even its
most traditional dialect can be understood without major problems by any
standard speaker.

A close analysis of ABS linguistic features does not seem to suggest that
this language was a creole. However, in order to offer a more comprehensive
picture of the issue, a sociohistorical analysis of ABS will also be provided.

The rest of this chapter is divided in two main sections. The first section consists of a sociohistorical overview concerning the evolution of Afro-Hispanic languages in the Americas. The second section analyzes exclusively the Bolivian region and, in this way, tries to cast light on the origin of Afro-Bolivian Spanish.

2.5. On the Scarcity of Spanish Creoles in Latin America

The paucity of Spanish-based creoles in the Americas has long been a hot topic of discussion in contact linguistics. In fact, if we consider the territories colonized by Spain in the "New World" and weigh them against those belonging to other European powers (e.g., French, English), we notice immediately that the density of creole languages is comparatively much lower than that found in former French and British colonies. There are only two languages that have been traditionally classified as Latin American Spanish creoles: Palenquero, spoken by the inhabitants of San Basilio de Palenque (Colombia), and Papiamentu, found in Aruba, Bonaire and Curacao (Dutch Antilles). Furthermore, it must also be said that also for these two languages the debate concerning their origin is far from over, since several scholars have argued that these languages should not be seen as Spanish creoles, but rather as Portuguese-derived varieties, which were subsequently relexified with Spanish lexicon (for a detailed account, see Goodman 1987; Jacobs 2008, 2009a, b; Martinus 1989; McWhorter 2000; Schwegler 1993).

The rest of the contact varieties that developed from the African Diaspora to Spanish America in colonial times did not give birth to creoles; rather, these languages resemble Spanish quite closely, and even if they are usually highly stigmatized from a social point of view, their grammars do not deviate radically from the standard language.

A variety of models have been proposed to account for the lack of Spanish creoles in the Americas. Some linguists have suggested that Spanish creoles did not develop, in contrast with other European varieties, because the social structure encountered in Spanish America was radically different from the one found in the French and British empires. In particular, the master-slave relation was by far less harsh: working conditions were presumably less strenuous; manumission was easier to obtain; and interracial relations were much more common.[4] These factors would have provided easier access

---

4. Schwegler (personal communication) disagrees with the idea that the slave-master

to the language spoken by the masters so that the acquisition of Spanish by slaves could take place without much difficulty (Laurence 1974, Mintz 1971).

Another common reason offered to account for the lack of Spanish creoles, at least in the Spanish Caribbean, is that the islands conquered by the Spaniards did not develop a large-scale plantation economy until the nineteenth century, so that the ratio between Europeans and Africans remained low for several centuries, which allowed for the acquisition of Spanish by the enslaved group. Only after the nineteenth century, the presence of blacks in these regions is more significant, but at that point the Spanish language was well in place in the colonies and could be acquired by the newly imported Africans (Chaudenson 1992, 2001; Laurence 1974; Megenney 1985; Mintz 1971).

Mintz (1971) clearly indicates that the reason for the non-creolization of Spanish in the Caribbean, in contrast with the creolization of English and French in the same region, has to do with the different ways in which social structure had been designed by the colonial authorities. He compares Spanish Cuba to French Haiti in the following way (1971: 488):

> In such colonies as Cuba, where one may suppose that a pidgin language did exist, at least briefly and in those periods when the influx of multilingual slave shipments was considerable, Spanish would provide a continuing medium of communication for culturally creolized slaves and freemen of all physical types. For the greater part of Cuba's and Puerto Rico's post-conquest history—that is, from the Discovery until at least the eighteenth century—the relative proportions of slaves to freemen were low, and the rates of manumission apparently high. In such colonies as Saint Domingue, where the importation of slaves after 1697 was both massive and rapid, the stabilization of a pidgin and the emergence of a creole language thereafter would be expectable, even though manumission was common,

relation in Spanish America radically differed from what was encountered in other European territories in the Americas. Nevertheless, I have to say that sociohistorical evidence seems to confirm this traditional distinction (see Andrés-Gallego 2005). In Sessarego (n. d.), I elaborate further on this idea. The analysis is based on legal data. The Spaniards, in fact, inherited the institution of slavery from the Roman *Corpus Juris Civilis* and elaborated on it over time, thus shaping the institution of slavery into a model much more flexible than the original Roman one. On the other hand, England, France, and Holland did not receive the institution of slavery in ancient times; there were no slaves in these European countries by the time the Americas were discovered. As a result, these colonial powers had to create a slave law from scratch, and oftentimes they borrowed directly from Roman law. As a consequence, their slave laws were much harsher than the one implemented in the Spanish colonies (see Watson 1989).

and the growth of an intermediate and economically influential free mulatto class—probably bilingual—was swift. Revolution and independence at the close of the eighteenth century, and the substantial elimination of the French colonists, may have contributed powerfully to the full stabilization of the Haitian Creole thereafter.

Laurence (1974) provides a similar account. The author offers a general description of slave life in the Caribbean regions belonging to Spain, France, and England. Laurence concludes that overall the Hispanic slave enjoyed much higher living standards. She indicates a list of elements that were in place in Spanish Caribbean but absent in the other colonies under investigation (i.e., French Haiti and English Jamaica): (1) Africans did not outnumber the Europeans; (2) manumission and interracial marriages were common; (3) for several centuries the economic structure of these regions was based on small-scale farms, where oftentimes poor Spaniards and free blacks worked side by side with the enslaved population.

Lipski (1987, 1993, 1998, 2000) also appears to support the idea that Spanish did not creolize in the Caribbean because of the socioeconomic characteristics of the region. He indicates that probably after the sugarcane boom of the nineteenth century the conditions for a creole language to emerge were in place in some of the biggest estates; however, the recently arrived slaves did not creolize the language already in place in the colony, so that the following generations learned Spanish natively.

McWhorter (2000) admits that these hypotheses may justify the lack of a full-fledged Spanish creole in the Caribbean; nevertheless, he argues that the aforementioned sociohistorical description cannot be applied to Spanish mainland colonies (e.g., Mexico, Colombia, Peru, Ecuador, and Venezuela), where—in his view—large-scale *haciendas* were in place and harsh working conditions were well attested (Blackburn 1997). McWhorter (2000) proposes that the lack of access to the lexifier language could not have been the reason for the development of creoles in the "New World," in contrast with Chaudenson's (1979, 1992) and Mufwene's (1996) analyses. In fact, if that were the case, we would then expect to find creoles in many former Spanish colonies, such as the Department of Chocó (Colombia), Chota Valley (Ecuador), Veracruz (Mexico), Lima (Peru), and the Mocundo *hacienda* (Venezuela), but this is not what happened. Conversely, McWhorter suggests that the real reason behind the lack of Spanish creoles has to do with the fact that Spanish was the only European power without a colony in Africa from which to extract an enslaved labor force. In his view, creoles developed from pidgins, and should not be seen as transformed varieties of their European lexifiers. Therefore, since Spanish did not pidginize in Africa, there could not possibly be Spanish creoles in the "New World."

Lipski (2005, n. d.) does not share McWhorter's view on this issue. He claims that McWhorter's account does not explain why, if the socioeconomic scenario he describes is correct, a pidgin did not develop in such Spanish territories overseas, or why a Portuguese pidgin previously formed in Africa did not relexify and develop into a Spanish creole, as supposedly happened in the case of Papiamentu and Palenquero.

As for Venezuela, Díaz-Campos & Clements (2008) provide a sociohistorical picture of slavery that greatly diverges from the scenario described by McWhorter. The authors indicate that McWhorter uses the word 'Africans' to describe mulattoes and other racially mixed individuals who were born in Latin America and could speak Spanish natively. They also stress the importance of the Spanish Crown's monopoly on slave trading. In their view, this last factor greatly constrained the introduction of African slaves into the colony. For this reason, the *bozal* sector of the population was never the majority, and a Spanish creole was not likely to develop in the region.

Conversely, other scholars have suggested that Spanish creoles did exist in the Americas (Bickerton & Escalante 1970; Granda 1978; Schwegler 1993, 1996), but over time they decreolized and disappeared almost everywhere, thus surviving only in San Basilio de Palenque and in the Dutch Antilles. However, it seems unlikely that such a language was once used so widely and then disappeared entirely, without leaving more substantial traces (Laurence 1974; McWhorter 2000).[5]

A linguistic feature that has been identified as a potential creole indicator for an Afro-Hispanic dialect is the grammatical element *ele*, found in Chota Valley Spanish (CVS). Schwegler (1999), in fact, suggested that *ele* should be analyzed as a Portuguese third person pronoun. In his view, *ele* offers undeniable evidence of a previous Afro-Portuguese creole stage for this language. However, this hypothesis has been challenged by Lipski (2009), who provides linguistic data indicating that Chota Valley Spanish *ele* might

---

5. Schwegler (personal communication) points out that his analysis of Palenque indicates that this might not have been the case. In fact, as Schwegler & Morton (2003) have shown, Black Spanish (as found in Palenque) does not contain the expected creole features. That is, speakers, in spite of three centuries of bilingualism and intense code-switching, have not transferred creole features into their Spanish. This fact, according to the authors, indicates that a creole language could have been spoken in other regions of the Americas without leaving behind any trace.

not have been derived from a Portuguese pronoun; rather, it would be the result of a paragogic process encountered also in other CVS words (*ayer à ayere* 'yesterday'; *ser à sere* 'to be'). Furthermore, the sociohistorical evidence also seems to suggest that the creole hypothesis for CVS is rather unlikely (Sessarego 2013).[6]

A potential creole root has also been claimed for Barlovento Spanish by Álvarez & Obediente (1998). The authors, in fact, suggest that this Afro-Venezuelan dialect presents some grammatical features that could hint at a previous creole stage (e.g., deletion of the copula verb, non-inverted order in questions, etc.). The basis for this claim would be that these phenomena are not generally encountered in Spanish sub-standard dialects, and that they should therefore be attributed to decreolization. Díaz-Campos & Clements (2008) have argued against this hypothesis by showing that the sociohistorical and linguistic data available for Barlovento Spanish do not seem to support a creole hypothesis for this dialect. First of all, they show that blacks were not sufficiently numerous in the area for a creole to emerge. Secondly, they provide an alternative account for all the features classified by Álvarez & Obediente as potentially inherited from the creole, by indicating that they are actually better explained in terms of imperfect second language acquisition, in a context in which the superstrate language was relatively available to the African slaves.

More recently, Lipski (2006a, b; 2007; 2008) has proposed that Afro-Bolivian Spanish (ABS) might be seen as the result of a decreolization process. As we mentioned in the introduction, Lipski indicates that ABS could be the descendant of a colonial Afro-Hispanic pidgin (2008: 186). In fact, he (2006b) suggests a possible creole origin for this vernacular. Lipski, however, recognizes that this claim is not supported by robust sociodemographic evidence, and for this reason, he does not reject *a priori* the hypothesis that ABS represents "a stable but not creolized variety of Spanish that co-existed with Highland Bolivian Spanish since its inception" (2006b: 37).

---

6. It must be said that Schwegler (1999) also provides data for Palenquero and nineteenth-century Cuba/Puerto Rico Bozal Spanish, where *ele* and *elle* are found respectively. The author maintains that these pronouns cannot possibly have been derived from their corresponding Spanish forms. To the skeptics who may consider *ele* as a simple paragoge of Spanish *él > ele*, he answers that plural *ele* in Palenquero provides evidence that the Spanish hypothesis is flawed, since paragoge of Spanish *ellos/ellas* 'they' could not give rise to Pal. *ele* (Schwegler 1999: 243–245). As far as the origin of Cuba/Puerto Rico Bozal *elle* is concerned, Schwegler indicates that it would be the result of a 'blend' between Afro-Portuguese *ele* and Span. *ella*, *ellos*, and *ellas* (1999: 250). Because of space limitations, I will not discuss this issue further here. Sessarego (2013) provides a more detailed account on the nature of *ele* in Chota Valley Spanish and a sociohistoric and linguistic analysis testing the feasibility of an Afro-Portuguese creole spoken in colonial Spanish America.

In the rest of this chapter, I will try to cast light on this issue. The socio-historical and linguistic data I was able to collect do not appear to indicate that ABS was once a creole that went through a decreolization process. On the contrary, the evidence collected seems to support the idea that it never creolized. This analysis tries to locate Afro-Bolivian Spanish in space and time with respect to the colonization of Spanish America. In doing so, it will also provide a detailed account of the sociohistorical conditions that led to the development of this Afro-Hispanic contact variety.

2.6. Black Slavery in Bolivia

Black slavery lasted in Bolivia for almost four centuries. It was introduced in the region with the Spanish conquest, in the first decades of the sixteenth century, and remained there until 1826, when immediately after the war of independence slaves were declared free. Nevertheless, the formal abolition of slavery, in practice, did not provide freedom to Afro-Bolivians. In fact, former slaves had to live on the lands belonging to the plantation and continued working there for a minimal wage until the Land Reform, which took place in 1952. This system was called *peonaje*; the salary provided to peons was so low that workers had to borrow money in order to survive; the debt was passed down from generation to generation, so that the socio-economic conditions of blacks did not improve and forced labor persisted. Only after the Land Reforms did Afro-descendants become free people and acquire the right to vote and to receive an education (Crespo 1995).

Brockington (2006) describes the black Diaspora to Bolivia as a forced migration that took place in two main phases. The first phase (roughly 1530–1650) was characterized by the arrival of black slaves and freemen, who participated in the many Spanish campaigns of invasion and conquest during the sixteenth and the seventeenth centuries. These people proceeded primarily from Spain and from other American colonies under Spanish control (e.g., the Caribbean). These first blacks to enter the Andean territory were typically identified with the term *ladinos,* which meant they had learned the Spanish customs, were Christians, and could speak Spanish fairly well. Over time, the situation changed. The second phase (1650–1830) saw an increase in the number of *bozales* introduced into the region. The newcomers were people imported to replace the shrinking native labor force. They were mainly used as domestic servants, farmers, and occasionally miners.

This chapter analyzes these two phases with the goal of shedding light on the currently unclear origins of ABS. Even though Afro-Bolivian slavery appears to have been a highly controversial and variable business, at least from a legal point of view, certain features of this tragic historical period seem to have been fairly constant across the centuries throughout the Bolivian territory.

In fact, black slavery in this Andean region was characterized by several elements, which indirectly provide us with key information about the possible means of communication adopted by the slaves. The linguistic picture emerging from the analysis of these sociohistorical facts seems to suggest that an Afro-Bolivian creole was not likely to develop and that the black population encountered in the territory could speak Spanish—or a good approximation of it—as a result of relatively good access to the language spoken by their masters. Such features can be briefly summarized as follows:

a. The slave trade was monopolized by the Spanish Crown, which kept the black/white ratio relatively low (Díaz-Campos & Clements 2008).[7]

b. The location of Bolivia, in the heart of South America, made the introduction of African slaves into this region a particularly difficult endeavor. The higher cost of slaves, deriving from such a geographical barrier, severely limited their importation (Klein 1986; Wolff 1981).

c. Spaniards in Bolivia did not need as much of an African workforce as elsewhere in the Americas. The indigenous population could be forced to work for a minimal wage, a scenario that was economically more profitable for the owner than investing in expensive African slaves (Bowser 1974; Mellafe 1984).

d. The combination of (a), (b) and (c) strongly constrained the introduction of Africans to the territory. As a consequence, massive importation was never reported, and rare were purchases of more than ten slaves at a time (Bridikhina 1995a; Busdiecker 2006; Crespo 1995; Lockhart 1994).

These are the main elements that characterized black slavery in the Bolivian region for a period of almost four centuries. The following sections

---

7. As we will see, a low black/white ratio was the general tendency. However, this does not exclude the possibility that in certain regions at certain points in time Afro-descendants might have been the majority of the population.

will focus on the two phases of the African Diaspora to the Bolivian territory to provide a better account of the potential genesis and evolution of this Afro-Hispanic language.

2.6.1. FIRST PHASE:
FROM THE SIXTEENTH TO THE MID-SEVENTEENTH CENTURY

The territory of the South American region now known as Bolivia was colonized by Spain during the sixteenth century. The conquest took place on two different fronts. The Spaniards penetrated the territory from both the west (via Peru) and the east (via Paraguay). Colonization, from the Peruvian side, can be schematically summarized as follows: in 1528, the Spanish conqueror Francisco Pizarro arrived by boat in Tumbes. By 1532 Spaniards reached Cajamarca and killed the Inca emperor Atahualpa. In 1533 they took Cuzco, the capital of the Inca Empire (Lockhart 1994). In 1538 they founded La Plata de la Nueva Toledo, now known as Sucre. In 1542 they settled Cochabamba, and by 1546 Potosí, the richest silver mines of Latin America. In 1548 they founded La Paz.

From the Paraguayan side, the conquest took place in a similar way. By 1537, Asunción, the current Paraguayan capital, was settled by the conqueror Juan de Ayola. Several explorations followed; in 1548 Spaniards settled Guapay, and a year later the Spanish captain Ñuflo de Chávez reached the already settled city of La Plata de la Nueva Toledo. The same captain founded the city of Santa Cruz in 1561, and in 1565 the explorer Diego de Villaroel founded Tucumán, in present-day Argentina (Klein 1999).

By 1559, La Plata de la Nueva Toledo (Sucre) became the capital of the Audiencia of Charcas, which had jurisdiction over the region roughly corresponding to present-day Bolivia, Paraguay, and northern Argentina. This was the provincial court that administered the large silver mines at Potosí. It belonged to the Viceroyalty of Peru until 1776, when it became part of the newly created Viceroyalty of Río de la Plata.

Africans played an important part in the conquest, pacification, and settlement of the Andean region. In the early reports of the conquest of the Andes, black servants appear on several occasions. Soon after discovering Tumbes, Pizarro returned to Spain to seek military and financial support for his conquering enterprise. In 1529, he was granted royal support and, among other things, received fifty-two black slaves free from duty charges (Bowser 1974: 4). Several other conquerors and settlers were given similar permissions to import a certain number of blacks. According to Bowser (1974), between 1529 and 1537 the kings released at least 363 import licenses, of which 258 were given to Pizarro and his relatives.

During this early colonial phase, the Spanish kings provided importing licenses to trustworthy settlers to import black slaves for military purposes and for the building of roads, bridges, and public infrastructures. These early black slaves who entered the Andean region were for the most part *ladinos,* professed the Catholic religion, spoke Spanish, and were familiar with the European ways. Usually they came from Spain or from already settled Spanish colonies (Bowser 1974: 3). The Spanish Crown and the Roman Catholic Church were committed to Christianizing the New World and were concerned with the introduction of potential enemies of the faith.

In these early times, before the New Laws of 1542–43, which established that Indians could not be made slaves, some Central American natives were taken as servants to Bolivia. However, even though these Indian slaves were not from the Andes, they could blend more easily and socialize with the local populations than blacks. African descendants, on the other hand, have always been perceived by the Indians as foreigners; they could not integrate easily into the local context, and for this reason they often identified more with their masters. This situation led to a reciprocal hostility between the Indians and the Africans, which turned out to be greatly beneficial to the Spaniards—and also partially to the blacks. Bowser (1974: 7) comments on the fact that blacks soon came to occupy an intermediary social position between the Spanish colonizers and the natives. Blacks were often used to repress Indian uprisings or to help local priests and *corregidores de indios;*[8] moreover, since they were expensive, they came to symbolize economic wealth and many Spaniards wanted to possess them as domestic servants to show economic status and acquire prestige in society (see Lockhart 1994).

Differently from other European powers, the Spanish Crown almost never encouraged the massive importation of slaves to the American colonies, especially to Bolivia. Slave trading dynamics in Spanish America were not regulated by a free market economy; conversely, the Crown highly constrained this business by granting only a few *asientos* 'import licenses' to a few trading companies and by charging buyers *almorjarifazgos* 'import taxes' and *alcabalas* 'sales taxes on following slave transactions.' Such a strict regulation played an important role in limiting the introduction of Africans into Spanish America. This kept the ratio between the black and the white

---

8. Spanish public officers who had legal power over Indian communities.

populations relatively low in several mainland colonies (see, for example, Díaz-Campos & Clements 2008 for Venezuela; Sessarego 2011 and 2013 for Bolivia and Ecuador).

There are no government censuses providing an account of the black population in Bolivia for the sixteenth century; nevertheless, from the letters sent by Spanish settlers to the Crown we can infer that many restrictions were in place regarding the introduction of African slaves into the region. In fact, in several instances the kings refused to grant *asientos*; often times this happened for financial reasons (Bowser 1974). A clear example is that of Pedro Cornejo de Estrella, a Spaniard who settled in Potosí. De Estrella urged the Crown to provide him with the licenses to import 150 black slaves free from royal taxes. He explained to the Crown that these workers would be fundamental to the exploitation of the gold resources of the Carabaya region, in line with a mining plan that he had specifically designed for such mines. However, the kings replied to De Estrella that he could introduce one hundred slaves at most into the region, and only half of them would be free from charges.

In other cases, the *asientos* were never conceded. For example, Viceroy Marqués de Cañete in 1556 asked the Crown to ship three thousand blacks to the colony. In order to recover the financial costs, he proposed that some of the slaves be sold to private miners. The remaining group would be used in the Chachapoyas mines. The Crown refused to send the slaves because this would have implied a costly and risky operation. Cases like this are crucial in understanding the dimensions of the slave trade in Spanish America, and particularly in Bolivia. In fact, this territory was farther away from Africa than the Caribbean region or the other coastal colonies, and it was reasonably populated by Indians, who could be exploited without having to take financial risks.

The journey that slaves were forced to undertake to get to Bolivia was extremely strenuous. In fact, slaves were sent from Africa and from Spain to the most important mainland harbor of Spanish America, Cartagena de Indias, Colombia. From there, they were resent by boat to the Atlantic coast of Panama. Once in Panama, they were forced to cross the isthmus to reach the Pacific side of the country. From the Pacific coast, they were shipped again, and after a long sea journey they reached the port of Callao, Peru, or Arica, Chile. Before getting to Bolivia, slaves had to walk from these two cities across the Andes (Busdiecker 2006; Klein 1986; Wolff 1981). The geographical barriers related to this strenuous journey implied that the slaves taken to Bolivia had to go through a significantly longer trip than those transported to the Latin American coastal regions. This element in all likelihood resulted in a higher number of black deaths (Busdiecker 2006; Klein 1986).

In the last decades of the sixteenth century, slaves started being introduced into the region through a route linking La Paz to Tucumán and Buenos Aires (Argentina). This last city, in fact, received slaves proceeding from Africa and Brazil. This second route was illegal and thus free from royal duties; merchants managed to introduce slaves from Argentina by corrupting local government officials (Bridikhina 1995a; Busdiecker 2006; Wolff 1981).

It can be said that the introduction of Africans into the Andes was not an easy task; these logistical problems inevitably resulted in a higher price for the slaves sold in Bolivia. In this Andean region, it is rare to find massive acquisitions of blacks by a single buyer (Busdiecker 2006). Legal documents confirm that a purchase record of more than ten slaves at a time was very unusual (Crespo 1995; Lockhart 1994). Owners who possessed many slaves acquired them progressively, usually purchasing only a couple of them at a time (Bridikhina 1995a; Busdiecker 2006).

Spain saw huge potential for exploiting Bolivian mineral resources from the very beginning of its conquest. For this reason, from early times, the economic structure of the region relied heavily on the mineral sector, and only in part on the agricultural one. In particular, Spaniards understood the importance of producing coca leaves, a product that for centuries has been used to help miners resist fatigue at high altitudes.

The conquerors mainly relied on the native labor force by adopting the *mita,* a pre-Colombian working system, according to which each Indian man would be assigned a certain task in line with a specific revolving schedule. In this way, all members of the community participated in the system, and once they had worked their designated shift, they were not required to work another one until all members completed their turn.

The *mita* was particularly demanding for the natives. On several occasions the royal administrators tried to reduce the workload on the Indians by suggesting that blacks substitute for them; however, these attempts were almost never successful. The massive employment of Indians in the mines was implemented during Viceroy Toledo's government (1569–80). In the case of Potosí, in 1578, it was established that 14,248 men would serve each year in the *cerro rico* mines (Bowser 1974). It is unlikely that within the *mita* system a creole language spoken by African slaves could have emerged, at least in the mining centers of the colony. Records of the time show that in such areas

Table 2.4
Demographic Figures for the City of Potosí (Crespo 1995: 26–29)

Year	Afro-Descendant Population	Total Population	Afro-Descendant Population (percentage)
1611	6,000	160,000	3.74 %
1719	3,206	70,000	4.58 %
1832	1,142	224,000	0.51 %

blacks were never a significant percentage of the population, as indicated in Table 2.4 (Crespo 1995).

Brockington reports a document written in 1618 by Antonio de Barranca, the archbishop of the Mizque-Santa Cruz diocese. The religious man describes the population statistics for baptismal data of six parishes under his administration. He indicates the presence of 250 *negros*, 150 *mulatos*,[9] and *zambos*,[10] 2,600 *yanaconas*,[11] 8,500 Indians, and 1,800 Spaniards. These data show an overall 3.8 percent Afro-descendant population (Brockington 2006: 176). Brockington also points out that the cost of buying a slave was much higher in Bolivia than Argentina. For example, a small slave child was sold at a price of 200–300 pesos in Mizque, while for the same amount of money an adult slave could be bought in Buenos Aires (Brockington 2006: 144). Therefore, also in several agricultural regions like Mizque-Santa Cruz, by this time, the probability of creole formation is quite slim.

In summary, several factors seem to have constrained the presence of black population in Bolivia during this first wave of importation (mid-sixteenth to mid-seventeenth century). We saw that the Royal Crown's monopoly limited the introduction of African slaves, the colony was not a plantation society, and Africans were usually employed as soldiers or domestic servants. The geographic location of Bolivia imposed higher costs on the introduction of Africans into the country; for this reason, the economic activities (mining and agricultural work) were mainly carried out by the native population employed through the *mita* system. Demographic evidence from Potosí and Mizque-Santa Cruz supports this scenario, indicating that overall the black population was a small minority.

9. Offspring of white and black parents.
10. Offspring of black and Indian parents.
11. Tribute-paying Indians.

2.6.2. SECOND PHASE:
FROM THE MID-SEVENTEENTH TO THE MID-TWENTIETH CENTURY

As we observed for the previous phase, several factors limited the introduction of a black workforce into the Bolivian region: the Spanish Crown's
monopoly of slave trading did not favor the importation of Africans, the
geography presented logistical barriers, and the availability of Indians
did not incentivize the employment of black workers, as they were comparatively more expensive. These elements affected the dimensions of the
African Diaspora in Bolivia also during the second phase, which lasted
approximately another two hundred years (1650–1850).

Even during this second phase, when the Indian sector of the population had drastically shrunk as a result of European diseases and strenuous
working conditions, the number of blacks introduced into the colony never
achieved the levels observed in other American regions. Slavery, however,
lasted for a very long time: it was officially abolished after the independence
from Spain (1827), but only in 1952, with the Land Reform, did Afro-Bolivians become free people.

There are not precise demographic figures, offering an accurate picture
of the evolution of the Afro-population in the territory over time. However,
Table 2.5 can provide us with a rough breakdown of the Bolivian population during the years 1650–1950 (see Rosemblat 1954; Crespo 1995; Pizarroso
Cuenca 1977; Dalence 1975).

The data presented in the Table 2.5 cannot give us a perfect analysis of
the evolution of the different ethnic groups. Nevertheless, they can at least
offer us a general idea. Data appear to suggest that the Afro-descendant
population has always represented a small minority, and its members never
outnumbered whites. Moreover, it has to be remembered that after the
abolition of slavery in 1851, blacks were no longer officially acknowledged,
making the reconstruction of their presence in the territory much more
complicated. Recent unofficial estimations of the Afro-Bolivian descendants suggest that the total approximate number should be 15,800, close to
0.18 percent of the entire Bolivian population (see Angola-Maconde n. d.,
reported in Lipski 2008: 30–31).

During this second phase, the Bolivian economy continued to rely in
good part on the mining activities and only partially on the agricultural sector. As we noticed in the previous sections, the Afro-descendant population
of the mining centers was a very small minority. Nevertheless, it must be
acknowledged that during this period, blacks could commonly be found in
the main Bolivian urban centers. In fact, because of their high value, Afro-

Table 2.5
Bolivian Population, 1650–1950[a]

	Blacks	Mulattos[b]	Mestizos[c]	Whites	Indians	Total
1650	30,000	5,000	15,000	50,000	750,000	850,000
1846		27,941		659,398	701,558	1,388,897
1940	7,800	5,000		870,000	1,595,000	2,900,000
1950		7,000	5,000	907,709	1,660,467	3,019,031

a. Sources: Rosemblat (1954); Crespo (1995); Pizarroso Cuenca (1977) for years 1650–1846; Dalence (1975) for years 1940–1950.
b. Offspring of white and black parents.
c. Offspring of white and Indian parents.

descendants came to symbolize economic wealth. As a consequence, the richest members of the society purchased some slaves, who were systematically shown in religious ceremonies or in other public celebrations to the rest of the community (Crespo 1995). Even though having black domestic servants was a common practice among the highest class, the percentage of Africans in Bolivian towns never achieved the levels found in other cities throughout Latin America. A clear case is offered by the 1778 census from Oruro, which reports 229 Afro-descendants, less than the 0.3 percent of the population. Another example is a census from eighteenth-century La Paz, where out of a total population of 40,000, only 350 were listed as blacks (less than 0.9 percent). (Busdiecker 2006).

Being unsuitable for the cold mining highlands, African slaves not only were used as domestic servants in cities; in some cases, they were employed for agricultural and livestock work in several rural regions of Bolivia. In particular, they were used in Mizque to produce wine and sugar, and in Los Yungas, where they were used to produce coca, crucial for the support of the flourishing mining industry in the highlands. In the next two sections, we will focus on the available sociohistorical evidence to determine the feasibility of a creole hypothesis for these two regions.

2.7. Black Slavery in Mizque

Brockington (2006) casts light on new data regarding a Jesuit *hacienda* in the province of Mizque in 1767. The agricultural enterprise used 134 black slaves. They were divided in two different groups: the married (including children) and the bachelors. The first group consisted of 110 slaves, who formed 29 households. The second one was composed by twenty-four adult men. Almost half of the slaves were *bozales*, while the rest were *criollos*. The *bozales* proceeded from Sierra Leone (67 percent), from Congo and central-south Africa (28 percent), and from west Africa-Dahomey and Senegabria (5 percent). Several elderly people are indicated in the Jesuits' reports. Brockington (2006) suggests that probably, when slaves became too old to work, they were manumitted to avoid paying property taxes. Interestingly, several slaves were older than forty-eight and one was recorded as being seventy-one.

From the available data, it is impossible to draw clear conclusions about the language spoken by these slaves. In fact, we do not know how many Jesuits and Indian workers were present on the *hacienda*. The presence of some older individuals, and the existence of many nuclear families, could indicate an environment with less harsh treatment and where local demographic reproduction was incentivized, as typical of Jesuits' plantations (see Macera 1966 for Peru; Bouisson 1997 for Ecuador).

We do not possess a detailed account of the different ethnic groups living and working in the aforementioned *hacienda*. In order to obtain a better understanding of the local situation, we may rely on the demographic figures provided by Francisco de Viedma, the governor of the province Cochabamba-Santa Cruz in 1788. The data in Table 2.6 indicate that the Afro-descendant sector of the population rose from 3.8 percent in 1618[12] to 6.4 percent in 1788, but never outnumbered the white-*mestizo* population (48.5 percent).

The town of Valle Grande hosted the largest *mulato-negro* group, 38.7 percent (3,243); followed by Cochabamba, 7.9 percent (1,775); Santa Cruz, 6.6 percent (150); Cliza, 6.3 percent (2,386); Mizque, 22 percent (672); Tapacarí, 3.8 percent (1,013); Sacaba, 3.5 percent (270); Ayopapa, 1.9 percent (249); and Arque, 1.4 percent (519) (see also Brockington 2006: 177–179).

Viedma's census does not provide us with data concerning the black population in the Yungas at that time. However, an important piece of information about this tropical region is encountered in the Jesuit document presented by Brockington (2006). The Yungan valleys are mentioned as a possible destination for three slaves that used to be employed by the Jesuits.

---

12. The territory covered by the 1618 baptismal statistics (by Antonio de Barranco) for the Mizque-Santa Cruz dioceses coincides almost entirely with the governmental province Cochabamba-Santa Cruz.

Table 2.6
Racial Distribution of the Population of the Provinces of Cochabamba and Santa Cruz in 1788[a]

City	Total Number	Racial Category					
		Spanish	Mestizo	Cholo[b]	Indian	Mulatto	Black
Cochabamba	22,305	6,368	12,980	0	1,182	1,600	175
Sacaba	7,614	1,249	2,290	0	3,805	269	1
Tapacarí	26,937	3,277	6,280	1,597	14,770	996	17
Cliza (Mizque)	37,615 (3,031)	6,682 (643)	12,192 (825)	0 (0)	16,355 (891)	2,366 (672)	20 (0)
Arque	22,137	1,238	3,936	1,286	15,158	496	23
Ayopapa	8,637	1,275	1,493	0	5,620	247	2
Valle Grande	8,373	2,995	1,918	0	217	3,215	28
Santa Cruz	10,578	4,303	1,376	2,638	2,111	0	150
Total Number	144,250	27,387	42,465	5,521	59,218	9,189	416
Percentage of Total	100.0	19.1	29.4	3.8	41.0	6.4	0.3

a. Source: Descripcion geografica, AGN, Sala 9, Intendencia, 5.8.5, Aug, 10, 1793. This is the original manuscript on which the subsequent Bolivian publication was based and where several of the population figures were printed incorrectly (Larson 1998: 175).
b. Officially defined as a person of one-quarter white ancestry and three-quarters Indian ancestry.

To conclude, we explored the available information concerning slavery in the Mizque region around the eighteenth century. The records that we have for the Jesuit *hacienda* in 1767 indicate that a substantial number of slaves were used in the region. However, these data do not imply that a creole language was employed in the plantation, especially if we analyze them keeping in mind Viedma's census, which suggests that the overall percentage of Afro-descendants for the region was probably too low for a full-fledged creole to develop.

2.8. Black Slavery in Los Yungas

After having provided this general account of black slavery in Bolivia, we now will describe the valleys where ABS is still spoken: Los Yungas, in the Department of La Paz. A precise reconstruction of when African slavery was introduced in this region has never been provided. However, several historical hints appear to suggest that the first significant black presence in this area probably appeared sometime in the early nineteenth century. For example, in an accounting report dated 1805, an overseer of a Yungan *hacienda*, Francisco Xavier de Bergara, states that the Marquesa de Haro was probably amongst the first landlords who used blacks in the region (Crespo 1995: 123–27).

Portugal Ortiz (1977: 78) mentions numerous documents concerning small slave transactions for this period. His data suggest that it was common for local owners to sell or purchase no more than one or two slaves at a time. An example is the case of an eighteen-year-old girl, who moved to Los Yungas in 1773. In this record it is said that she was originally purchased in Potosí, and after residing in Oruro for a while, with her last owner, she was now sold to a new master to work in the tropical valleys. Another case in 1761 is the purchase of a married couple from Angola by a priest living in Chulumani (1977: 78). These small transactions, concerning only a couple of slaves at the time, support Bridikhina's (1995a), Crespo's (1995), and Lockhart's (1994) view regarding the high price of slaves as a powerful constraint on the massive employment of a black workforce (see also Busdiecker 2006). According to them, masters who possessed several slaves often accumulated them over a long period of time. This could be the case for Don Antonio de Tejada, who at the time of his death (1806) owned forty-one slaves in a Yungan *hacienda* (Portugal Ortiz 1977: 80–81).

Pizarroso Cuenca (1977: 74) retells the local story of "King Bonifacio," who apparently sometime around the beginning of the seventeenth century was proclaimed king of the black community by the slaves of the Mururata *hacienda*. According to this story, after the arrival of a new group of slaves at the plantation owned by the Marqués Pinedo, some of the blacks already working there realized that one of the newcomers was the king of their African tribe. They could not tolerate such a humiliation for their king. For this reason, they agreed with Marqués Pinedo to work extra hours to free him. The slaves also built him a house, and the freed slave came to be known as King Bonifacio Pinedo or Negro Bonifaz. We cannot tell for sure if this story really happened; however, the coronation must have taken place, since this black monarchy is still in place in the Afro-Bolivian community. The part of the story that may raise some doubts is not if the coronation happened, but rather when. In fact the date indicated as 1600 could have been reported wrongly since neither documents nor records of any kind indicate significant African presence in Los Yungas by that time. Besides, Portugal Ortiz notes that, by the eighteenth century, the Yungas was only partially colonized. The Coroico area was taken for the first time from the "*enemigos ynfieles*"[13] to be given to Don Buena Aventura Joseph Rodríguez, in 1736 (Portugal Ortiz 1977: 76). As the Mururata *hacienda* borders Coroico, and the distance between the two villages is no more than an hour's walk, it is unlikely that one could have been colonized more than 136 years before the other.[14]

The first available piece of documentation reporting the existence of black slavery in Los Yungas is a church record concerning the death of a *mulato* in 1703 in the village of Chicaloma. Leons (1984) indicates that the limited availability of documents reporting Afro-descendants records until the beginning of the nineteenth century is due to the limited number of slaves in the region until that point. The first document providing concrete information on the black population in the Yungas is from the early nineteenth century. Crespo (1995: 96) raises a question about the relative proportion of black labor employed in agriculture and provides the following answer:

> Talking about Yungan *haciendas* in the Department of La Paz, not all of them used this kind of workforce, and at least in some regions of this area, those that employed it were a minority.

13. Non-Christianized Indians.

14. Moreover, if the colonization proceeded from La Paz, Mururata would hardly have been conquered before, because it is located after Coroico.

Crespo (1995: 96) quotes a letter written by the Chirca priest in 1802, where he accounted for the percentages of blacks and Indians in twenty-three local *haciendas*. Of these *chacras*,[15] only four were employing a black workforce; that is, in Guayraoata 15 *negros* or *mulatos* out of 65 workers; in San Agustin 17 out of 28; in Yacata 23 out of 128; and in Collpar 28 out of 142. Crespo also adds that in 1802, Ocabaya, Yungas, had a population of 32 blacks, 80 *mestizos*, 94 Spaniards, and 643 Indians. No other data are available for the Yungas until 1883. For this year, comprehensive information concerning the demographics of whites, Indians, *mestizos*, and *morenos* (a term that includes *negros*, *mulatos*, and *zambos*) is disclosed for two *haciendas*: Pacallo and Mururata, where the highest concentration of *morenos* is found. Pacallo had 67 whites, 63 *mestizos*, 340 Indians, and 56 *morenos*; Mururata numbered 55 whites, 183 *mestizos*, 236 Indians, and 324 *morenos*. Moreover, without specific mention of ethnic group separation: Chulumani with 14 *morenos* out of a total of 220 inhabitants; Tajmo, Calupre, Chigno, Chimasi, Tolopala, Suquillo with 49 out of 902; Coroico with 113 out of 5,335; Impata with 252 out of 2,465; Coripata with 315 out of 3,867; Chupe with 240 out of 1,212; and Lanza with 102 out of 8,255.

The overall information available for these last *haciendas* suggests that the black population was not the majority. Even in Pacallo and Mururata, where the highest concentrations of Afro-descendants is found, the ratios of *morenos* to whites and *mestizos* combined (who supposedly spoke Spanish proficiently, being offspring of a Spanish mother or father) are 56:130 for Pacallo and 324:233 for Mururata. *Morenos* outnumber whites and *mestizos* only in Mururata. However, even here, the feasibility of a creole origin does not hold, as the majority of the slaves were probably made up of *criollos*, and the *morenos* not only included blacks, but also *mulatos* and *zambos*.[16]

Reports dating from the late eighteenth century show that Los Yungas did not host large-scale plantations; on the other hand, the most common cultivations were of a small and medium nature (Busdiecker 2006). Busdiecker (2006: 38) summarizes Soux's (1993) account of the labor force used in the Dorado Chico *hacienda* during that period. Apparently, not all the workers of Dorado Chico were slaves; rather, some were classified as *mingas* and some as *peones*. *Mingas* received a salary and were employed only when

---

15. Small pieces of land used for agriculture.

16. As the traffic of blacks was declared illegal in 1826 but was completely eradicated by 1848, it is likely that importations decreased significantly during this period of time. In this case, I agree with Singler (1992: 326), who argues that the faster the locally born population emerges, the more the resulting contact variety is influenced by the lexifier (see Arends 2008 for a detailed account on the role of demography in creole formation).

extra help was needed. *Peones,* on the other hand, did not receive money for the work they did in the *hacienda;* however, they were provided with a parcel of land and three days off a week to cultivate their own products. Finally, there were enslaved workers, who usually were not provided with land; they had to work for free and were given food, clothes, and wood, since they had no material means to achieve such provisions by themselves (see also Crespo 1995).

Health conditions for Yungueños have always been an issue: lack of hygiene, insects, and a variety of tropical diseases often caused the death of many workers. This fact represented huge problems for the local landlords, for whom the death of a slave consisted of a complete capital loss (Busdiecker 2006). For this reason, whenever possible, planters would prefer to employ Indian labor. These considerations concerning the use of black slaves and free workers are reported by the *hacienda* overseer mentioned above, Francisco Xavier de Bergara. In an analysis called *Demonstraciones matemáticas* 'Quantitative evidence,' de Bergara tries to show that using enslaved workers was not financially convenient and that relying on free Indians would have been more lucrative. The overseer mentioned a list of factors that were at the root of this situation. His final objective was to persuade the *hacienda* proprietor, Don Antonio Sáez de Tejada, to sell his slaves and replace this labor force with natives. Bergara's observations indirectly provide us with a good idea of the social patterns encountered in the Yungas at that time. Masters had to feed and clothe their slaves; moreover, they had to provide them with an accommodation and Christian education.

De Bergara estimated a cost per-capita of 1.5 reales[17] a day. In addition, the master also had to pay for Church rites, including weddings (12 pesos) and funerals (12 pesos). Moreover, blacks were more likely to rebel, and therefore extra overseers were needed to control a group of them. Catching a runaway slave could cost anywhere from 25 to 100 pesos, while the death of one of them, often from diseases, would have represented the loss of the total investment. Apparently, in Sáez de Tejada's *hacienda* workers received the same daily wage independently of whether they were African descendants or Indians: three reales for the men and two reales for the women and the children. Nevertheless, it is important to keep in mind that slaves implied an initial capital investment (360 pesos per man and 410 per woman), while native workers did not imply such a cost because they were free.

17. One peso consists of eight reales.

As Busdiecker (2006: 38) points out, in Dorado Chico all workers (*mingas, peones,* and slaves) were supposed to receive equal payment. In practice, however, only *mingas* received money; the rest were generally given provisions (e.g., corn, potatoes, etc.) (see also Soux 1993). According to de Bergara, part of the issue with using enslaved workers had to do with the many days off slaves had: seventy-nine a year, including Sundays and Catholic holidays. Besides, periods of pregnancy, illness, or just childhood would have implied lower production, which did not free the owner from feeding and clothing the slaves.

By analyzing de Bergara's description of Yungueño slavery, we immediately understand that black slaves were exploited for profit by their owners; however, the conditions in which they lived were probably not as harsh as those experienced by many other blacks in other enslaving societies in the Americas. This might have had to do with their higher prices in the region and to the fact that owners wanted to protect their costly investments. Also, two additional crucial aspects of African slavery in Spanish America, which differentiated it from black slavery in other European colonies, were the legal rights slaves could enjoy and the importance given by the Crown to the religious sphere of everyday slave life. Masters had to baptize their slaves and provide them with Christian education. By law, slaves could not work on Saturdays and during the religious festivities. If masters were caught violating such a requirement, they were forced to pay high fees (Watson 1989).

With that being said, some cases of mistreatment can be found. For example, legal documents of the seventeenth century record the case of a group of slaves that escaped from an owner in Potosí. When they were captured, the tribunal established that the reason for their flight was hunger and the poor treatment endured by the slaves. However, the court decided to punish the blacks with fifty whippings, even though it could be proven that they did not steal anything from their master (Crespo 1995: 21–26). Another case is that of a six-year-old girl from La Paz whose owner damaged her eye and broke her arm (Bridikhina 1995b: 60).

Cases of violent black resistance were rarely encountered in Bolivia. A slave rebellion took place in Mururata in 1795, and the *hacienda* owner, Ignacio Pinedo, had to call army troops to suppress the uprising. A similar act of resistance happened again in Mururata in 1805; while in 1809 Santa Cruz experienced another case of collective revolt (Busdiecker 2006).

Busdiecker (2006: 41) indicates that even if violent uprisings were not common, blacks usually tried to pursue freedom in other ways. For example, they resorted to legal means to change owners in case of mistreatment.

Crespo (1995) suggests that paying for one's freedom must not have been easy because of the reduced salary received by the slaves. However, Portugal Ortiz (1977: 78) shows that this was a widespread practice. An example he mentions is that of Juan José Nieto (1795), who paid Antonio Sáez de Tejada (Yungan owner) 400 pesos to free him. Portugal Ortiz relates that, in order to find the money, Nieto asked Don Pedro Oquendo for a loan, promising him that he would have paid it back in four years (100 pesos a year). This and other evidence provided by Portugal Ortiz, in addition to the story told about Rey Bonifaz (Pizarroso Cuenca 1977), suggest that the Bolivian *hacienda* was probably a fairly flexible system if compared with other enslaving societies elsewhere in the Americas.

In summary, the historical evidence collected seems to indicate that Los Yungas were settled and colonized only around the eighteenth century. The only clue that may suggest a previous settlement is the orally-told story of King Bonifacio. In fact, as reported by Pizarroso Cuenca (1977), the legend would indicate that a significant African workforce had already been introduced in the Yungas by 1600. However, no data reporting African presence in the Yungas by that time is known. On the other hand, historical documents confirm that by 1736 the region had yet to be completely colonized and the employment of black workers was not massive: small slave transactions and a relatively small ratio between blacks and whites appear to have characterized the African presence in this area. Moreover, Bonifacio's coronation indirectly indicates that manumission was possible in the Yungan community. It also has to be stressed that the social conditions encountered in Los Yungas seem to have been less harsh than those found in many other regions in the Americas. In fact, the Yungan *hacienda* was not a large-scale plantation society; rather, it was organized into small and medium farms; blacks were not always slaves but rather *mingas* and *peones*. Slaves represented a costly investment to slave owners, and the Spanish legal system provided slaves with a variety of civil rights. For these reasons black Yungueños were probably treated less brutally than many other slaves in other American colonies. Finally, manumission was relatively common.

2.9. Conclusion

This chapter has provided linguistic and sociohistorical considerations to investigate the possible origins of Afro-Bolivian Spanish. A closer look at the linguistic features proposed as potential indicators of prior creolization (Lipski 2008) indicates that the grammatical elements found in Afro-Bolivian Spanish can be encountered in advanced second languages or non-standard Spanish and Portuguese dialects for which a creole hypothesis is not feasible. Therefore, the presence of such features in Yungueño Spanish does not imply a prior creole stage for this variety.

The sociohistorical data analyzed do not suggest a creole origin either. Several factors have affected the dimension of African slavery in Bolivia and consequently the presence of black population in the territory from the sixteenth century through the middle of the twentieth century. In fact, the Spanish Crown's monopoly of slave trading, the geographic location of Bolivia and the availability of a native workforce affected the cost of Africans, raising their price and, as a result, reducing the number and the dimension of slave transactions. The non-massive introduction of a black workforce into the territory favored the acquisition of a closer approximation to Spanish by the slaves.

ABS is a contact language presenting several key differences from standard Bolivian Spanish; however, even in its most basilectal variety, this dialect would be perfectly intelligible by any standard Spanish speaker. ABS is therefore a vernacular that derived much of its structure from Spanish, but which, at the same time, carries on morphological simplifications and regularizations. These elements seem to be the remaining traces of crystallized second language strategies, rather than the evidence of a more radical creole existence.

The commonalities between traditional ABS and standard Spanish would hardly be the result of a change that took place in the last fifty to sixty years, especially because the speakers of this vernacular are elderly people who were at least thirty years old when the Land Reform (1952) occurred. As a consequence, they did not experience any formal education and spent their entire life in these rural Yungan communities, where they continued to carry out agricultural work. Claiming a decreolization, in this specific case, would imply that these people since the Land Reform had such an intensive contact with standard Spanish that they could learn a very close approximation to it at an already advanced age and, at the same time, abandon almost completely their creole-like mother tongue. This is not a likely scenario.

The core of Chambers' theory maintains that "the standard dialect differs from other dialects by resisting certain natural tendencies in the grammar and phonology" (Chambers 2003: 254). Chambers pushes the model as far as to say that "the basilectal form is primitive, part of the innate bioprogram, and the standard form is learned, an experiential excrescence on the bioprogram" (2003: 286). I am not sure of whether in cases of standard L1 acquisition such a radical view can account for all the features that he indicates as 'vernacular roots' (see Chambers 2003: 129); however, for the case of contact varieties like ABS, we can say that certain forms are easier to learn/process than others, and unless social pressure rules them out, there should be no reason why they could not normally crystallize becoming part of the core grammar of the language natively acquired by following generations.

Los Yungas provided the perfect place for such a crystallization to take place, as they were isolated, rural valleys far from the social pressure posed by formal education, standardization, and the linguistic norm. Note that my claim does not imply that after the Land Reform ABS did not experience a process of approximation to the standard variety. This is something that I am not questioning, and that is clearly visible by looking at the evolution of inflectional morphology across generations (Delicado-Cantero & Sessarego 2011; Sessarego 2009; Sessarego & Gutiérrez-Rexach 2011, 2012). What appears to be less convincing is that Afro-Bolivian Spanish could have been a radical creole before 1952 that underwent a drastic decreolization after that date.

This recent approximation to standard Bolivian Spanish further supports the claim of Vernacular Universals. In fact, when the factors preserving the traditional dialects began to disappear—essentially after 1952—the pressure, imposed by standardization and the linguistic norm, pushed Afro-Bolivians towards dropping the traditional dialect in favor of the more prestigious Spanish variety. Sociohistorical and linguistic evidence suggests that ABS was not the descendant of an Afro-Hispanic pidgin; rather, it should be seen as a vernacular, which carries the undeniable traces of second language acquisition processes, and from its inception resembled Spanish quite closely.

Language Variation and the Minimalist Program

3.0. Introduction

Traditionally, generative hypotheses have mainly been built on standard language data, on the basis of the grammaticality judgments of a few speakers. This approach has proven very powerful in producing a remarkable number of generalizations, which were formulated by excluding all variability complications due to performance and by exclusively focusing on native speakers' syntactic intuitions (Barbiers 2009: 1608). On the other hand, such a methodology has often been criticized by sociolinguists, who base their observations on much larger corpora of naturalistic production data, and have developed several techniques to study the 'real vernacular,' or the language spoken by people when paying no metalinguistic attention to their speech (Labov 1972). In the last decade, works on microvariation attempted to combine these previously contrasting approaches to compare a speaker's intuitions with real production data, with the goal of developing more empirically-testable generalizations (Cornips & Poletto 2005). Recent works within the minimalist framework entail a derivational approach that is inconsistent with parameter-based accounts. Thus, an extension of the parameter/microparameter idea to individual variation seems to not be a straightforward matter (Adger & Smith 2005).

This chapter provides an overview of the major approaches proposed in the literature to deal with inter- and intra-speaker variability. In doing so, it highlights the importance of the present work in combining the formal and the sociolinguistic methods to obtain a more fine-grained account of the syntactic phenomena characterizing the Afro-Bolivian Spanish Determiner Phrase.

3.1. Accounting for Variation

Inter- and intra-speaker variability has long been a hot topic of linguistic debate. Typically, formal linguists have considered such a variability as an instance of E-language, thus not concerning the core syntactic competence of the speaker and therefore, for the most part, ignorable. On the other hand, a different response, radically contrasting with the former, grew within the variationist/sociolinguistic paradigm. It consisted of positing variable rules (e.g., Cedergren & Sankoff 1974; Labov 1972), where probabilities would be built into the notion of grammar. Other models stipulated multiple grammars, where speakers have several parametric configurations (Henry 2005; Kroch 1989, 1994). Finally, a more recent account (Adger 2006; Adger & Smith 2005; Parrott 2007), developed within the architecture provided by the Minimalist Program (Chomsky 1995, 2001, 2006) and the study of microparametric variation (Barbiers & Cornips 2001; Kayne 1996, 2000; etc.), postulates that variation is the overt result of covert lexical selections. Such a model claims that there is a reduced available number of syntactic operations (Merge, Move, Agree), which are universal and constant, while the elements entering the syntactic numeration can vary in feature specification. The following sections will provide a brief overview of these competing accounts.

3.2. Approaches to the Study of Language Variation

3.2.1. THE FORMAL APPROACH

Mainstream syntactic theories (Chomsky 1957, 1965, 1986) have given little room to the study of inter- and intra-speakers' speech variability. Within the formal approach of Principles and Parameters (P&P) (Chomsky & Lasnik 1993), languages can essentially be seen as combinations of a finite set of innate principles, which are shared by all varieties, and a set of binary parameters that are responsible for the syntactic variability observable across human languages. Within this framework, principles are "language-invariant statements" (Chomsky 1995: 25), whereas parameters must be set for certain values. Principles are part of a genetically innate Universal Grammar (UG), which all humans possess. As such, they do not need to be learned through exposure to language. Rather, exposure to language merely triggers the parameters to adopt the correct setting.

Chomsky (2000) compares the language faculty to a switch box. This box consists of two components: a fixed network, which is the innate principles of language, and several switches, which are options determined by experience, binary parameters that can be set on or off. Different parametric combinations lead to different grammars. In Chomsky's (2000: 8) words,

> When the switches are set one way, we have Swahili; when they are set another way, we have Japanese. Each possible human language is identified as a particular setting of the switches—a setting of parameters, in technical terminology.

According to the Principles and Parameters model (Chomsky & Lasnik 1993), children are assumed to learn the language of their parents or their social environment. During this process, acquisition can be imperfect, thus involving parameter resetting and therefore cross-generational language change. Chomsky & Lasnik's (1993) model does not allow parameter resetting during the lifespan of the speaker; in their view, once a parameter has been set, it is for good. For this reason, within the field of generative syntax, cases of language internal variation have often been disregarded as instances of E-language, not interesting from the perspective of scholars aimed to unveil the secrets of the I-language. As a result, formal syntactic theories have traditionally been built on partly-idealized standard languages, on the basis of grammaticality judgments of a reduced number of informants. As stated in the first section, parameter resetting or change is viewed in diachronic terms but never as a synchronic process.

As van Gelderen (2005: 180–181) pointed out, vast linguistic corpora have never been popular research tools among generative syntacticians. She reports Wasow (2002), who highlights Chomsky's negative attitudes on the employment of quantitative data, which in his view would not provide any useful insight into the knowledge of the I-language. Here is a quote from Chomsky (1962: 128):

It seems that probabilistic considerations have nothing to do with grammar, e.g. surely it is not a matter of concern for the grammar of English that 'New York' is more probable than 'Nevada' in the context 'I come from—.'

Needless to say, as we will see, sociolinguistic models of language variation have a radically different opinion on the issue.

3.2.2. THE SOCIOLINGUISTIC APPROACH

The Chomskyan revolution and its formal methodology produced a great deal of linguistic generalizations; the reason for its success can be found in its ability to put aside the variability derived from natural speech data, and its exclusive focus on the abstract intuitions of a restricted number of native speakers. Yet, for these same reasons, such a model has often been criticized by sociolinguists, who instead based their observations on bigger corpora of naturalistic production data, and developed several techniques to study the 'real vernacular', the real language spoken by people when paying no meta-linguistic attention to their speech (Labov 1972).

In the sixties, Labov (1969) extended the concept of optional rule, borrowed from the earlier transformational model (Chomsky 1957), to the idea that rules can be variable and dependent on several internal (linguistic) and external (extralinguistic) factors (Cornips 2006). In fact, Labov's 'variable rules' are based on the concept of 'orderly heterogeneity' (Weinreich, Labov, & Herzog 1968: 100), "the idea that variation in language is not random or free, but systematic and rule governed" (Tagliamonte 2006: 129). This notion of variable rules was first developed from the observation that people make systematic choices when they speak (Labov 1969). Because of such systematicity, statistical models can be developed; this implies postulating that language has a probabilistic component.

The sociolinguistic approach is founded on the principle of accountability (Labov 1966: 49). This principle states that all variants belonging to the same syntactic variable must be accounted for in the variable environment. In order to identify what should be considered as a variant of a specific variable, the synonymy principle (principle of sameness) must be followed. In other words, variants of the same variable are only those tokens that consist of "[different] ways of saying the same thing" (Labov 1972: 323).

Sociolinguists developed a variety of research tools that allow them to cope with the demands of their data (Chambers 2003). One of the most famous statistical instruments employed to analyze sociolinguistic variation is VARBRUL (by David Sankoff), which evolved in several more powerful software programs during the last decades (e.g., GoldVarb X by Sankoff, Tagliamonte, & Smith 2005).

Within the Labovian/sociolinguistic approach, variation has been at the center of attention for at least forty years; on the other hand, within the traditional Chomskyian/generative framework, it has generally been excluded from the research agenda, because it was considered to be a case of performance rather than competence. Nevertheless, in more recent years, scholars working within the generative framework have attempted to account for diachronic variation (Kroch 1989) and also to capture dialectal and interspeaker variation, exploring the notion of parametric variation and, in the last decade, fine-graining it to include so-called microparameters (Benincà 1989; Kayne 2000; among others).

3.2.3. THE DIACHRONIC APPROACH

Dating from the 1980s, the study of diachronic syntax has seen the rise of a particularly rich tradition of combining quantitative and formal perspectives (see Kroch 1989, 1994, for an overview). In Kroch's view, the historical evolution of competing variants in syntactic change parallels the evolution of morphological doublets. In both cases, the competition of two forms is diachronically unstable: "One form tends to drive the other out of use and thus out of the language" (Kroch 1994: 7). This parallelism would be explained by the existence of the "Blocking Effect" (Aronoff 1976). The blocking effect, in Kroch's words (1994:9), does not prevent doublets from arising in a language through social processes (e.g., language contact). Rather, it acts as an economy constraint on their storage.

Kroch supports his analysis of syntactic change by suggesting the general validity of the "Constant Rate Hypothesis" (Kroch 1989). The "Constant Rate Hypothesis" claims that usage frequencies change rates mirror the gradual substitution of one grammatical form by another. The formulation of the "Constant Rate Hypothesis" represents a key step toward the analysis of E-data. In fact, Kroch clearly states that statistical tendencies and patterns encountered in vast corpora can unveil the principle and parameters belonging to speakers' competence. Kroch envisions a theory of language variation that admits competing grammars. He proposes that diachronic change is triggered by variation between forms belonging to the competence realm. See also van Gelderen (2005) for an account of how the use of corpora has been integrated in syntactic theory.

3.2.4. THE MICROPARAMETRIC APPROACH

Besides these approaches to diachronic variation and change, there is also a recent and growing body of research that over the past decade or so has attempted to combine insight of generative linguistics with variationist analysis in the study of synchronic variation, especially across dialects of the same language (see Auger 1998; Barbiers 2005; Cornips & Corrigan 2005; Heap 2001; Kayne 1996, 2000; King & Nadasdi 1997; etc.).

Kayne (1996) was the first one to propose the notion of 'microparameter.' Microparameters represent the 'switches' that distinguish closely related languages. In Kayne's (1996: xii) words,

> Comparative work on the syntax of a large number of closely related languages can be thought of as a new research tool, one that is capable of providing results of an unusually fine-grained and particularly solid character. If it were possible to experiment in languages, a syntactician would construct an experiment of the following type: take a language, alter a single one of its observable syntactic properties, examine the result to see what, if any, other property has changed as a consequence of the original manipulation. If one has, interpret that result as indicating that it and the original property that was altered are linked to one another by some abstract parameter.

Obviously, such an experiment is impossible to carry out; however, by analyzing closely related varieties, one can achieve similar results. Recent syntactic dialect atlas projects, such as the ASIS and the SAND have undertaken such a challenge. These research projects have various objectives. They not only explore the geographic distribution of syntactic variables; they also correlate them to the investigation of language change and to the broader study of universal properties of the human language, to understand the loci and limits of syntactic variation within linguistic systems (Barbiers 2009). The great improvement of this new approach on previous ones is that past formal studies were primarily concerned with standard varieties, whereas microvariation research includes non-standard languages.

As Barbiers & Cornips (2001: 2) state,

> This [approach] does not only enhance the empirical basis of syntactic theory, but it also reduces the influence of prescriptive rules and makes it possible to test potential correlations between syntactic variables while keeping other, possibly interfering factors constant.

Weiß (2001), in fact, argues that standard languages, studied at school through formal instruction, may present quite unnatural prescriptive properties, often imposed by processes of standardization. Researchers working on this track acknowledge that dialects are heterogeneous systems, on the grounds that a dialect is constantly in contact with one or more standard varieties and sometimes also with other dialects (Barbiers & Cornips 2001: 2). Each individual may speak in a slightly different way, so that it is possible to postulate the existence of slightly different grammars and thus the existence of individual microparameters.

3.2.5. VARIABILITY IN THE MINIMALIST PROGRAM

Finally, a model that combines aspects of the microparametric framework, the sociolinguistic approach to data collection, and recent formal proposals concerning the architecture of language (the Minimalist Program) is the one presented by Adger & Smith (2005). This model, in contrast with previous formal accounts, seems particularly well suited for the study of intra-speaker variation. In fact, even in the most recent approaches to the study of dialectal variation, work on variability among the idiolects of individuals has been largely lacking. On the other hand, in Adger & Smith (2005) and related studies (e.g. Adger 2006; Parrott 2007), intra-speaker variability becomes the core of linguistic research, bringing previously disregarded phenomena, considered as belonging to E-language, to the forefront (Adger & Trousdale 2007).

The minimalist framework admits several phonological outputs for a given semantic interpretation. Adger & Smith (2005) argue for characterizing syntactic variation in terms of uninterpretable features. Certain uninterpretable features may be present in one category but absent in another. Since they are uninterpretable, they would have no semantic repercussion, thus being equally legitimate for a convergent derivation. Therefore, variation is reduced to the specification of the uninterpretable features in a derivation (Adger & Smith 2005: 161). As expected, syntax *per se* remains invariable or "perfect" (Brody 2003), given that variation is located only in the lexical component. Variation will occur when one item or another enters the numeration and takes part in a syntactic derivation. Several extralinguistic factors may affect the probability of accessing one lexical item or another: social environment, social class, gender, age, education, etc. (Adger & Smith 2005: 164).

Notice that this approach is different from Kroch's or Labov's alternatives in that variation is located in the selection of lexical entries. On the other hand, Kroch's model suggests that there is more than one system of grammatical knowledge available to the speaker, and variation depends on the speaker's selection of one or the other system. The Labovian variable rules approach contrasts with this in that it states that the variation is part of the rule, tying it in more directly to grammatical competence.

Within the framework proposed by Adger and Smith, there is no notion of a probability directly linked to a particular rule; the only possible rules (Merge, Move and Agree) are invariant and apply categorically in particular cases across languages. Adger and Smith's perspective differs from the previous approaches in that it assumes only one invariant grammatical system, containing universal mechanisms, rather than a range of systems. Overt variation is driven by the choice of different lexical items, which may be influenced by various internal and external factors. This may be considered as a "very minimal theory" (Adger & Smith 2005: 165), since the idea that speakers have to choose lexical items is one that cannot be avoided.

A concrete example of this proposal is the analysis of alternation between *was* and *were* in Buckie, a small fishing town near Aberdeen (UK). After providing accurate information on the methodology used to collect natural data and presenting quantitative analyses on internal and external factors affecting the alternation, Adger & Smith (2005) proposed a formal model to account for the results. Consider the following examples (Adger & Smith 2005: 154):

(7) Buckie English
  a. He says 'I thocht *you were* a diver or somethin.'
    'He said 'I thought you were a diver or something."
  b. Aye, I thocht *you was* a scuba diver.
    'Yes, I thought you were a scuba diver'

The verb form *was* instead of standard *were* appears 54 percent of the time; it can be found with all persons except *they*. In terms of syntactic derivation, pronouns bear certain interpretable features for person and number. In Adger and Smith's view, first and second person bear [+person], while third person is [−person], assuming that third person is lack of a positive specification for person (see, for example, Harley & Ritter 2002 and references therein). T bears unvalued features for number and person: T [tense: past, *u*case: nom, *u*num:, *u*pers:]. After merging with T, the pronoun *you* provides T with plural number and second person values, and the result is *you were*. If T is valued as third person, singular, the result is *he/she was*. Variation occurs once there is an alternative lexical item that could appear in the same syntactic context, with the same interpretable features, but with different uninterpretable ones. The authors propose the following alternative: T2 [tense: past, *u*case: nom, *u*pers:] (Adger & Smith 2005: 166), which lacks [*u*num:]. If T2 is selected, the derivation will remain the same except for the absence of specification for number. Since there is no specification for number in T, the verb form will be *was* by default even when the pronoun is second person plural. Therefore, this model provides a reasonable account for the variable grammatical phenomena encountered in Buckie by combining quantitative approaches to data collection and formal generative theories.

The postulation that overt variability is due to different lexical specifications, while syntax *per se* remains invariable, will be one of the assumptions of the present work. This will allow us to account for important cross-dialectal, intra-dialectal, and intra-personal instances of variation, while testing syntactic hypotheses and potential correlations between linguistic features and syntactic phenomena. In chapter 8, the study of gender/number agreement variability will provide a concrete example of how inter- and intra-speaker variation can be accounted for by Adger & Smith's approach. In particular, I will postulate the presence or absence of certain uninterpretable gender and number features across the ABS DP to capture the agreement variability encountered in the speech of my informants.

3.3. Variability across Closely Related Dialects: The Afro-Hispanic Case

In recent years, syntactic studies have devoted more and more attention to dialects and substandard varieties of different languages—e.g., Italian

(Benincà 1989, 1994; Poletto 2000), English (Adger & Smith 2005), Dutch (Barbiers & Cornips 2001), etc. So far, little attention has been paid to the study of microvariation across Spanish dialects; to my knowledge, a book has yet to be published on microparametric syntax concerning Afro-Hispanic contact varieties.

The majority of the dialects that developed in Latin America from the contact of African languages and Spanish in colonial times consist of vernacular varieties. The grammars of these languages are relatively close to the one of standard Spanish. Nevertheless, they clearly present the traces of second language acquisition strategies and contain a variety of constructions that would be considered ungrammatical in standard Spanish. It is exactly this close proximity to the standard language that makes these varieties so suitable to be analyzed with a microparametric approach.

3.4. Data Collection and Methodology

The fieldwork was conducted during July–August 2008, December 2009, and July-August 2010. More than fifty speakers were interviewed. They were Afro-Bolivians living in the communities of Tocaña, Mururata, and Chijchipa, three villages in the municipality of Coroico, North Yungas. Data collection was carried out through sociolinguistic interviews. In particular, speakers were asked to talk freely about a variety of topics, while the interviewer would take part in the conversation by asking follow-up questions (see Labov 1984).[1] The goal was therefore to reduce the Observer's Paradox (Labov 1972) as much as possible. Only later, usually after one or two days from the time of the interview, the same informant would be asked for grammaticality judgments. This specific technique (sociolinguistic interviews followed by grammaticality judgments) was adopted in order not to influence the results of the interview by altering the informant in advance on the linguistic phenomena that were being studied, thus trying to reduce his/her metalinguistic awareness.

A comparison of grammatical intuitions and sociolinguistic interviews can be very helpful in studying socially stigmatized dialects like Afro-

---

1. According to the Principle of Tangential Shift, interviews may be arranged into a network of topics that do not need to be followed according to a prescribed sequence. The conversation between the interviewer and the informant should start with the least personal questions and progress, step by step, towards more intimate topics. The shift between topics should be as smooth as possible. It should be based on follow-up questions to what has just been said by the informant.

Bolivian Spanish; nevertheless, the same methodology is not equally suitable for all linguistic phenomena. In fact, while the syntactic variability of high-frequency structures can be addressed efficiently by recurring to sociolinguistic interviews, less frequent constructions are better studied by asking informants for grammaticality judgments. Therefore, while a comparison between natural data and inducted elicitations has been a prerogative in the study of the Afro-Bolivian Spanish DP, this book also considers necessary methodological adjustments imposed by the nature of the different phenomena under study.

3.5. Conclusion

To summarize, this chapter has provided an overview of the main approaches proposed to account for language variability. I focused on recent developments within the field of microparametric syntax (Barbiers & Cornips 2001). In particular, I presented the framework suggested by Adger & Smith (2005), which combines quantitative analysis and formal theory. The present book will adopt such a model to study several syntactic aspects of the Afro-Bolivian Spanish Determiner Phrase.

Microparametric syntax is a growing research field, which can be employed to test formal theories, often designed on standard language data. While several microparametric generalizations have been provided for Italian, English, and Dutch dialects (see, for example, Adger & Smith 2005; Barbiers & Cornips 2001; Benincà 1989; Poletto 2000), such research has yet to be conducted on Afro-Hispanic contact varieties. This opens up a new field of investigation, which if addressed in a methodological and systematic way, could lead to interesting discoveries. One of the main goals of this study is to place the first stone in the foundation of such a research program.

4

From NP to DP

4.0. Introduction

The aim of this chapter is to present the most important issues concerning the generative study of the nominal domain and to provide an outline of frameworks and ideas that will be evaluated in the following chapters based on the empirical data encountered in Afro-Bolivian Spanish (ABS). The internal structure of the Noun Phrase (NP) became a central issue in syntactic investigation from Chomsky's (1970) remarks on nominalization, and especially after Abney's (1987) Ph.D. dissertation, which provided theoretical and empirical bases for the idea that the Determiner Phrase (DP) is the maximal phrase projected by the class determiner, which takes NPs as complements. This idea came to be known as the DP Hypothesis, and during the last four decades much research has been carried out with the aim to understand the configuration of the syntactic structure contained between D and N.

The rest of this chapter is organized as follows: Section 4.1 describes Abney's (1987) and Szabolcsi's (1983, 1987, 1989, 1994) works, which provided the first theoretical and empirical evidence for the study of DP. Section 4.2 presents an analysis of some of the key articles that have argued in favor of additional functional projections between D and N and N-movement to its surrounding layers; in particular, we will focus on the studies that appear to be the most pertinent to our analysis of the ABS DP. For this reason, we will concentrate on Num(ber)P (Ritter 1991), Gen(der)P (Picallo 1991; Ritter 1993), A(djective)Ps (Cinque 1990, 1993), thematic layers (Valois 1991), and nP shells (Carstens 2000). Section 4.3 illustrates Longobardi's (1994) analysis of DPs headed by empty Ds, and Chierchia's (1998) hypothesis concerning the status of bare nouns and full DPs across languages (Nominal Mapping Parameter). These last two proposals will provide us with a framework on which to test the nature of ABS 'bare' nominals.

4.1. The Determiner Phrase Hypothesis

4.1.1. ABNEY (1987)

In his Ph.D. dissertation, Abney (1987) develops the idea that a nucleus D, containing agreement features, precedes the nominal head, mirroring in this way the structure of the sentence, where Infl precedes V. He analyzes several languages in which the noun agrees with its possessor and suggests that NP is the complement of an element similar to Infl (D), which provides a position for agreement (AGR).

In order to show this parallelism between NP and VP (now DP and CP), Abney presents data from several languages like Yup'ik (a Central Alaskan Eskimo language), Tzutujil (a Mayan language), and Hungarian, among others. In Yup'ik, for example, all nouns agree with their possessors (8) and share with the verbs the same morphological AGR markers (9) (see Abney 1987: 28).[1] Moreover, both the subject of the NP and the subject of transitive verbs take ergative (ERG) case.

(8)

    a.   angute-m kiputa-a-Ø
            man-ERG buy-OM-SM
            "the man bought it"

    b.   angute-t kiputa-a-t
            man-PL buy-SG-PL
            "the men bought it"

    c.   angute-k kiputa-a-k
             man-DU buy-SG-DU
            "the men bought it"

---

1. SM stands for 'subject agreement marker'; OM stands for 'object agreement marker.'

(9)
    a.   angute-m kuiga-Ø
          man-ERG river-SM
          "the man's river"
    b.   angute-t kuiga-t
          man-ERG river-SM
          "the man's river"
    c.   angute-k kuiga-k
          man-ERG river-SM
          "the man's river"

Abney (1987) accounts for the parallelism between case-marking and agreement by providing parallel IP and DP structures.

(10)

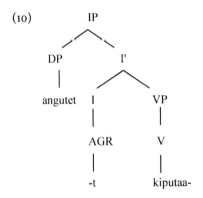

(11)

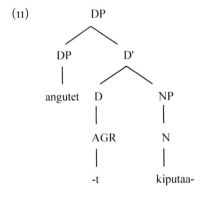

4.1.2. SZABOLCSI (1983, 1987, 1989, 1994)

Additional support for the parallelism between the nominal domain and the sentence domain is provided by Szabolcsi, who suggests that both the complementizer and the article are elements responsible for turning their complements into arguments. In fact, in Szabolcsi's view, differently from Abney's, DP does not equal IP, but rather CP (1994: 189). C and D are assumed to act as subordinators capable of receiving a Θ-role assignment. The case is illustrated in (12), where C (12a) may introduce an argument, while, conversely, C is not allowed in clauses unable to take on such a function (12b).

(12)

    a.   I think [CP (that) you are nice]

    b.   *[CP That you are nice]

Szabolcsi (1983: 89–92) claims that the structure of DPs in Hungarian mirrors the one of CPs. In fact, the possessive marker on Ns takes the place of the tense/mood morpheme on Vs (13), thus suggesting the existence of an Infl-like category in the nominal domain, as Abney (1987) will indicate a few years later.

(13)

    a.   Mari-Ø alud-t-Ø

         Mary-NOM sleep-PAST-3SG

         'Mary slept'

    b.   (A) Mari-Ø vendég-e-Ø

         The Mary-NOM guest-POSS-3SG

         'Mary's guest'

She hypothesizes the existence of two functional categories in the extended nominal projection. According to Szabolcsi, there are two nominal nuclei (14): a lower nucleus, (N), which assigns nominative case to its specifier, and a higher nucleus, (D), assigning dative case to its specifier; its lexical realization is the article, which turns nouns into arguments, mirroring in this way the function of CP in the extended verbal projection (15) (see Szabolcsi 1989: 2; 1994: 189).

(14)

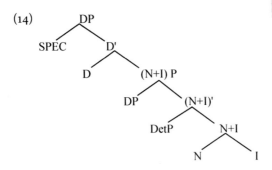

(15)

The reason for proposing this specific architecture is based on Hungarian data. In Hungarian, in fact, there are two different ways of expressing possession. In the first case, the possessor is marked with nominative case (16a), and extraction out of a DP is not possible (16d); in the other case, the possessor is assigned dative case (16b) and it can be extracted (16c). Szabolcsi (1994: 196) adopts the structure suggested in (16) to compare the process of possessor extraction to that of subject extraction.

(16)

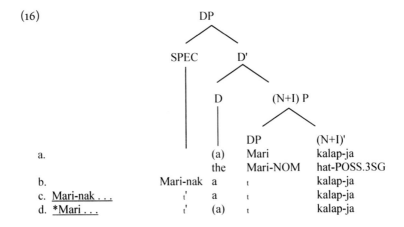

		SPEC	D	DP	(N+I)'
a.			(a)	Mari	kalap-ja
			the	Mari-NOM	hat-POSS.3SG
b.		Mari-nak	a	t	kalap-ja
c.	Mari-nak . . .		t′	a	t	kalap-ja
d.	*Mari . . .		t′	(a)	t	kalap-ja

In (16a) the possessor *Mari* takes the nominative case, the noun denoting the possessed object *kalap* carries the morpheme *ja*, which indicates agreement in number and person with *Mari*, a phenomenon parallel to subject-verb agreement in CP. N+I assigns nominative case to *Mari*, while the article *a* is located in D (but it is not compulsory). In (16b), the possessor *Mari* precedes the article *a* and receives dative case *nak*, while *kalap* presents the same morphological marking. As schematically shown in (16c, d), the possessor can be extracted when it is dative-marked, but it cannot when it is assigned the nominal case. SPEC-DP in (16b) parallels in this way SPEC-CP, from which subjects can be extracted too. The parallelism pointed out by Abney (1987) and Szabolcsi (1994) between nominal and verbal domains will be further investigated in following works (Cinque 1993; Longobardi 1994; Picallo 1991; Ritter 1991; among others) aimed at showing that the movement of N in DP mirrors the one of V in CP.

4.2. In between N and D

Several works argued for N to D movement in support of the DP Hypothesis. In this section, we will go through those that appear to be the most relevant to the study of the Afro-Bolivian Spanish Determiner Phrase. We will examine Ritter (1991, 1993), proposing the existence of the functional category Number (NumP). We will then summarize Picallo (1991), who postulates the presence of a Gender Phrase (GenP) in Romance; Cinque (1990, 1993), who provides a layered structure to account for adjectival projections; and finally, Valois (1991) and Carstens (2000), for an account of nominal Θ-role assignments and nP shells.

4.2.1. RITTER (1991, 1993)

Ritter (1991) was the first to suggest the presence of a functional projection corresponding to numeral marking. She argued that Num(ber)P is the complement of D in Modern Hebrew and in Romance languages. The argumentation in favor of a DP-internal functional projection Num(ber) P is based on two types of genitive constructions in Modern Hebrew. The first construction analyzed is the construct state (17), which shows a surface order derived by N-movement. In fact, she shows that the subject must asymmetrically c-command the object, and proposes that the noun raises from N to D, crossing over the possessor (18).

(17) Ahavat Dan et ift- o
love Dan ACC wife-his
'Dan's love of his wife'

(18)

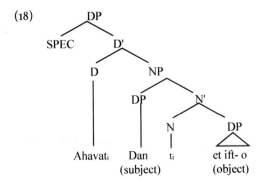

The reason for the proposal of an intermediate functional projection between D and N becomes clearer when we analyze the free genitive constructions in (19). In fact, example (19) cannot be accounted for by the structure adopted in (18). Assuming the validity of the head movement constraint (Travis 1984),[2] and that the definite article *ha* is located in D, an intermediate position between D and N, acting as a landing site for N, must be postulated. This category is called Num and projects a NumP, it contains the number specification of the NP. Ritter (1991: 43) claims that NumP is not only specific to free genitive constructions; rather, all nouns in Hebrew have it.

(19) Ha-axila šel Dan et tapuax
The-eating of Dan ACC the-apple
'Dan's eating of the apple'

---

2. THE HEAD MOVEMENT CONSTRAINT (Travis 1984, in Ritter 1991: 39): A head (X°) can move only to the position of the head (Y°) that properly governs it.

(20)

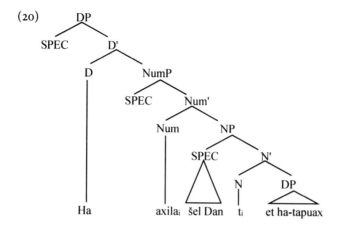

In a following analysis, Ritter (1993) elaborates also on the syntactic location of the feature 'gender.' She suggests that in Hebrew, nouns come from the lexicon with a specification for gender features, while in Romance languages the feature gender is located in Num and appears on N only as a result of N raising.

(21)   Hebrew
        [DP Det [NumP Num [NP   N]]]
                                  |
                         ... X-[gender] ...
        Romance
        [DP Det [NumP Num [NP   N]]]
                          |
                 ... Y-[gender] ...

The claim exemplified in (21) is supported by the fact that a switch in gender feature derives a new noun in Hebrew (22), while in Romance languages such a phenomenon is not as productive; rather, it is limited for the most part to Ns with human or animate reference (see Harris 1991).

(22)

		Masculine nouns		Feminine nouns	
a.	magav	'wiper'	magev-et	'towel'
	magav-im	'wipers'	magev-ot	'towels'
b.	maxsan	'warehouse'	maxsan-it	'magazine'
	maxsan-im	'warehouses'	maxsani-ot	'magazines'
c.	amud	'page'	amud-a	'column'
	amud-im	'pages'	amud-ot	'columns'

Additional support for the gender feature distinction between Hebrew and Romance languages is provided by the analysis of irregular plurals in these two varieties. While Hebrew plural affixes appear to be specified exclusively for number, Romance plural affixes seem to be specified for both number and gender. This last point is backed by the fact that a large number of irregular nouns in Romanian are masculine in the singular and feminine in the plural, as shown in (23).

(23)
  a. Un scaun confortabil e folositor.
     a(M.SG) chair comfortable(M.SG) is useful(M.SG)
     'a comfortable chair'
  b. Nişte scaune confortabile sînt folositoare.
     Some chairs comfortable(F.PL) are useful(F.PL)
     'Some comfortable chairs are useful.'

4.2.2. PICALLO (1991)

The idea that both gender and number features are checked under NumP in Romance is not shared by Picallo (1991), who suggests, based on Catalan data, the existence of an additional intermediate Gender Phrase (GenP) within the DP. This functional phrase would be located between NP and NumP (24), reflecting in this way the linear order of the morphemes attached to the noun stem. GenP would be justified because in Catalan (and in the rest of Romance languages) adjectives and determiners agree not only in number with N, but also in gender. Gender and number morpheme affixations would be the result of cyclical N-movement to the gender and number heads (24–25) (see Picallo 1991: 282–283).

(24) Catalan: les gates 'the cats'(F-PL)
     [DP les [NumP [[[[gat-]ı]+F]ȷ+PL][GenP tȷ [NP tı]]]]

(25)

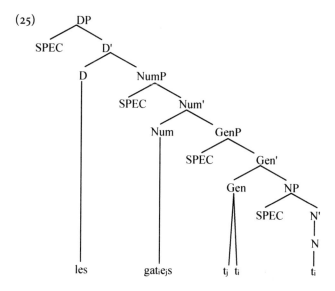

4.2.3. CINQUE (1990, 1993)

The parallelism between DP and CP seems to be further supported by the distribution of adjectives with respect to NP, which presents striking similarities with the distribution of adverbs with respect to VP. In fact, subj(ect)-oriented APs are followed by manner or thematic APs and preceded by sp(eaker)-oriented APs (26–27) (Cinque 1993: 24, see also Crisma 1990, 1993).

(26) ... [XP APsp-or _ [YP APsubj-or _ [ZP APmanner/themat _ [NP N ...

(27)
    a.   La probabile goffa reazione immediata alla tua lettura.
        'The probable clumsy reaction immediate to your letter.'
    b.   Probabilmente avranno goffamente reagito subito alla tua lettera.
        'They probably have clumsily reacted immediately to your letter.'

In line with this view, Cinque (1990, 1993) proposes that APs are universally generated to the left of N, in the SPEC of a limited set (six or seven) of functional projections between D and N. This is called the SPEC-hypothesis

(Cinque 1993: 26). For this reason, the different surface positions that As take across human languages are explained as the result of N-movement. To illustrate the differences between pre-nominal and post-nominal adjective location in Germanic and Romance languages, Cinque argues in favor of N raising to a functional head in Romance (but not in Germanic) (see Cinque 1993: 21).

(28) [D . . . [AP Y [AP N]]] (Romance)

(29) [D . . . [AP Y [AP N]]] (Germanic)

Cinque (1993: 25–30) shows that there are theoretical and empirical reasons to favor the SPEC-hypothesis over the hypothesis that analyzes APs as adjuncts (e.g., Picallo 1991; Valois 1991; Bernstein 1993). In fact, there is a specific ordering of APs that appear in the unmarked case, while adjuncts can appear more freely; thus the presence of adjectives on the left of N depends on the position of the specifiers in which they are base-generated. Another point in favor of the SPEC-hypothesis is that the number of adjective is limited, while there is no limit to the number of adjuncts.

4.2.4. VALOIS (1991)

In his Ph.D. dissertation, Valois (1991) argues in favor of a layered DP hosting functional projections capable of licensing Θ-role assignments, mirroring in this way the sentence structure (see Sportiche 1990). He claims a syntactic architecture in line with Giorgi & Longobardi's (1991: ch.3) Thematic Hierarchy, where the possessor is located in a higher projection, dominating the external thematic argument, which, in turn, is higher than the internal argument (30) (see Giorgi & Longobardi 1991: 117).

(30) Thematic Hierarchy: possessor > agent > theme

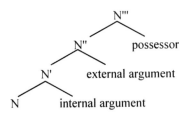

In particular, Valois adapts Sportiche's (1990) proposal on the layered structure of VP to the nominal domain. He indicates that direct objects are sisters to their Θ-marking head and that Head-movement of X to X* is required to license the external Θ-role (31) (see Valois 1991: 7). XP* is projected only if the external Θ-role is assigned. In the presence of a possessor, an additional PossP is projected, thus resulting in the more articulated structure provided in (32) (see Valois 1991: 16).

(31)

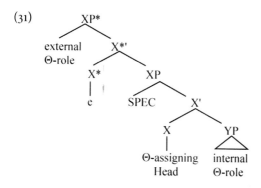

(32)

The structure in (32) reflects the Thematic Hierarchy in (30). Valois supports this architecture by showing how "higher arguments may bind lower ones but not vice-versa" (1991: 17) and how extraction operations out of Noun Phrases are conditioned by this argument linearization, where an agent cannot be extracted when co-occurring with a possessor, and a theme cannot be extracted if it co-occurs with either a possessor or an agent (1991: 19). He shows these contrasts on extraction by presenting three sets of examples (33–35). As it can be observed, only the higher constituent (which appears underlined) can be extracted yielding grammatical constructions (see Valois 1991: 20).

(33) Possessor higher than agent
    a.   La photo de ce photographe de <u>ce collectionneur</u>.
          AGENT   POSSESSOR
          'This photographer's picture of this collector.'
    b.   *Le photographe dont je connais la photo de <u>ce collectionneur</u>.
          'The photographer of-whom I know this collector's picture.'
    c.   <u>Le collectionneur</u> dont je connais la photo de ce photographe.
          'The collector of whom I know this photographer's picture.'

(34) Agent higher than theme
    a.   La photo de <u>ce photographe</u> de du Louvre.
          AGENT   THEME
          'This photographer's picture of the Louvre.'
    b.   *Le musée dont je connais la photo de <u>ce photographe</u>.
          'The museum of-whom I know this photographer's picture.'
    c.   <u>Le photographe</u> dont je connais la photo du Louvre.
          'The photographer of-whom I know the picture of the Louvre.'

(35) Possessor higher than theme
    a.   La photo du Louvre de <u>ce collectionneur</u>.
          THEME   POSSESSOR
          'This collector's picture of the Louvre.'
    b.   *Le musée dont je connais la photo de <u>ce collectionneur</u>.
          'The museum of-whom I know this photographer's picture.'
    c.   <u>Le collectionneur</u> dont je connais la photo du Louvre.
          'The photographer of-whom I know the picture of the Louvre.'

4.2.5. CARSTENS (2000)

Carstens (2000) builds on the Thematic Hierarchy proposed by Giorgi and Longobardi (1991), and adopted by Valois (1991), and suggests that NPs are surrounded by several thematic layers headed by a light noun 'n,' which projects its corresponding nP shell. In this way, the nominal domain would parallel the verbal one, where the VP is dominated by a vP shell headed by a light 'v' (Larson 1988; Hale & Keyser 1993). In Carstens' model, thematic roles are assigned to nominal arguments under nP. In line with Chomsky's (1995) analysis of external verbal arguments, Carstens (2000: 320–321) argues that nominal agents are base-generated in the SPEC-nP of a shell above the NP core; moreover, agents are asymmetrically c-commanded by possessors and both asymmetrically c-command themes (36).

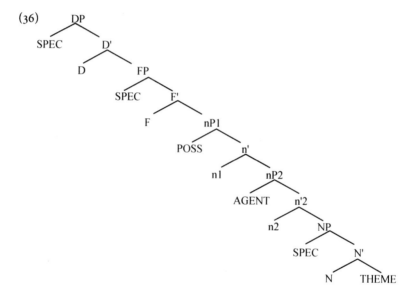

4.3. The Status of NPs and DPs

In this section, I analyze two proposals concerning the nature of DPs and NPs across languages (i.e., Longobardi 1994; Chierchia 1998). These studies will provide us with a theoretical framework on which to test the status of 'bare' argumental nouns in Afro-Bolivian Spanish.

4.3.1. LONGOBARDI (1994)

Longobardi claims that "a 'nominal expression' is an argument only if it is introduced by a category D" (1994: 620) and therefore that a "DP can be an argument, [an] NP cannot" (1994: 628). This is because nominal expressions are essentially predicates, they provide a description of a certain nominal entity, but they do not refer; determiners do. In fact, Ds act as operators selecting (or binding) a specific variable out of the given NP set (see also Contreras 1986).

The author builds his hypothesis on Germanic and Romance language data; Longobardi (1994: 609–610) points out that pronouns, proper names, generic nouns, and common nouns show different syntactic behaviors and thus occupy different syntactic positions. Pronouns are base-generated in D, and therefore can act as arguments. Generic and proper nouns are base-generated in N and may rise to D via N-to-D movement in the syntax (for Romance) or at LF (for Germanic). Common nouns cannot occupy a D position; they are essentially predicates, which need to co-occur with either a pronounced or a null D category in order to yield a semantically interpretable argument. This implies that a bare common noun in argument position is not actually 'bare'; rather, if the noun is not accompanied by a pronounced D, then there must be a silent determiner in the structure.

An empty D is subject to lexical government; the noun co-occurring with it receives an indefinite/existential interpretation with a generic reading (Longobardi 1994: 617–618). What has just been suggested may be exemplified by the Italian examples given in (37–38), where argumental common nouns can appear 'bare' (with an empty D) only when they are morphologically plural (*marocchini* 'Moroccans') or mass (*acqua* 'water') and when they are lexically governed (in this case by a verb). Under these conditions, they receive an indefinite/generic interpretation unspecified for number (Longobardi 1994: 615).

(37)
a. *Acqua viene giù dalle colline.
     water comes down from the hills
b. Viene giù acqua dalle colline.
     comes down water from-the hills
     'Water comes down from the hills.'
c. Ho preso acqua dalla sorgente.
     have taken water from the spring
     'I took water from the spring.'

(38)

    a.   *In questo ufficio marocchini telefonano sempre.
        in this office Moroccans call always
    b.   In questo ufficio telefonano sempre marocchini.
        in this office call always Moroccans
        'In this office Moroccans are always calling.'
    c.   In questo ufficio incontro sempre marocchini.
        In this office I meet always Moroccans
        'In this office I always meet Moroccans.'

4.3.2. CHIERCHIA (1998)

The idea that only DPs can act as arguments is not shared by Chierchia (1998), who proposes a semantic parameter, the Nominal Mapping Parameter, to account for the distribution of bare NPs and DPs across languages.

Chierchia (1998: 400) divides human languages into three main groups. In languages of group 1 (e.g., Chinese/Japanese), NPs are, by default, arguments and do not act as predicates [+arg, −pred]. As a result, they cannot be counted without the insertion of a specific operator, ∪. In group 1, languages show no definite articles; nouns are deprived of number morphology and their default interpretation is 'mass.' NPs in group 2 languages (e.g., Romance Languages) show the opposite values [−arg, +pred], meaning that they are essentially predicates and can act as arguments only if a D element is inserted. Nouns in these languages inflect for number and the count/ mass distinction is specified at the lexical level. In the last possible language group (e.g., Slavic/Germanic languages), NPs are [+arg, +pred]. This means that they both can be arguments and predicates. Mass and plural count nouns can appear in the argument position and the application of a "down" operator (∪) shifts them to a predicate position. Conversely, predicates can be shifted to the argument position by recurring to the "cap" operator (∩), which turns them into kind terms. In addition, Chierchia suggests that languages lacking definite articles recur to the null "iota" operator (i), which essentially acts as a functional item of this kind. On the other hand, if a language has an overt determiner capable of performing such an operation, *iota* should not be available since it would be more natural to use the overt element.

5

Semantic and Syntactic Properties of "Bare" Nouns

5.0. Introduction

This chapter provides an analysis of bare nouns in Afro-Bolivian Spanish (ABS), whose nominal domain does not fit the typological categorization sketched by Chierchia's (1998) Nominal Mapping Parameter. After considering the mass/count, kind, and indefinite/definite readings of ABS bare nouns, it is suggested that these categories are not structurally bare; rather, they are embedded in a DP, headed by an empty D nucleus (in line with Longobardi 1994). Data suggest that cover determiners encode a variety of type-shifting operators, which are conditioned by several pragmatic, semantic, and syntactic factors. Given the nature of the phenomenon under study in this chapter, the use of sociolinguistic techniques and quantitative analyses did not appear to be the most appropriate. All the examples reported are the result of elicitations and grammaticality judgments.

As reported in chapter 4, it is generally accepted that NPs (Noun Phrases) are predicates while DPs (Determiner Phrases) are arguments (Longobardi 1994; McNally 2004), at least in Romance languages. A great deal of research has been carried out recently to refine Chierchia's proposal, which would account for the distribution of bare plurals and full DPs cross-linguistically. As indicated in section 4.3.2, Chierchia divides human languages into three main groups, whose nominal domains can be schematically represented as follows: (A) [+arg, −pred] (e.g., Chinese/Japanese): generalized bare arguments, every (lexical) noun is mass, lack of plural morphology, generalized classifier system; (B) [−arg, +pred] (e.g., Romance Languages): count/mass distinction, lack of bare NPs in argument position, plural morphology; (C) [+arg, +pred] (e.g., Germanic/Slavic Languages) count/mass distinction, bare mass nouns and plurals in argument position, lack of bare singular count nouns, plural morphology. Chierchia also predicts that languages lacking an overt definite article would recur to a silent iota operator, a semantic operator acting as a definite article. On the other hand, if a language has an overt definite article, iota will not be available.

Such a proposal has been empirically challenged by Déprez (2001) for Haitian French, Schmitt & Munn (2003) for Brazilian Portuguese, Baptista (2007) for Cape Verdian Portuguese, and Kester & Schmitt (2007) for Papiamentu, among others. Another language that does not fit Chierchia's Nominal Mapping Parameter is Afro-Bolivian Spanish (ABS), where bare nouns—deprived of plural morphology—can appear in both subject and object positions and are subject to a variety of interpretations depending on the context in which they are found.

5.1. ABS Nouns and Chierchia's Nominal Mapping Parameter

The typological classification provided by Chierchia's (1998) Nominal Mapping Parameter does not seem to be able to account for the ABS nominal configuration. In fact, ABS is endowed with definite articles and plural morphology, nouns are specified for count and mass at the lexical level, and bare singular nouns can appear in both subject and object positions.

Let us start with an analysis of plural morphology. Number (plural/singular) is usually conveyed by the determiner heading the DP, which can be inherently plural (e.g., *lu*, see 39), or can carry the inflectional plural marker–*s* (40).

(39)
    a.   Lu chico boliviano.
          the-PL guy-SG bolivian-SG
          'The Bolivian guys.'

    b.   El chico boliviano.
        the-SG guy-SG bolivian-SG
        'The old good friend.'

(40)
    a.   Sus caramelo bonito.
        his-PL candy-SG good-SG
        'His good candies.'
    b.   Su caramelo bonito.
        his-SG candy-SG good-SG
        'His good candy.'

As can be observed, the nominal and the adjectival stems remain bare, so that plural marking appears only on determiners (see Delicado-Cantero & Sessarego 2011). Moreover, ABS Ns are specified for count and mass at the lexical level. This point is clearly shown in (41), where, given the same context—and the same quantifier, *mucho* 'much/many'—two different nouns take on different readings: *vino* 'wine' as mass, *vaso* 'glass' as count.

(41)
    a.   Mucho vino tomó Pablo a la boda.
        much-PL wine-SG drunk Pablo to the-SG wedding-SG
        'Pablo drunk so much wine at the wedding.'
    b.   Mucho vaso tomó Pablo a la boda.
        much-PL glass-SG drunk Pablo to the-SG wedding-SG
        'Pablo drunk so many glasses at the wedding.'

Furthermore, ABS Ns can appear bare, in both subject and object positions (42). As we will see, they can take on a variety of readings, as a function of their syntactic environment and pragmatic context.

(42)   Chancho come papa.
       pig-SG eat potato-SG
       'Pigs eat potatoes.'

However, in contrast to other languages in which argumental plural bare nouns are found (e.g., Brazilian Portuguese [BP]), in ABS, as we have seen, nouns never inflect for number in the traditional dialect, and therefore, they cannot carry plural morphology. These data indicate that, again, contrary to Chierchia's predictions, there are languages in which singular count bare nouns can be arguments, while plural ones are not allowed. Lastly, ABS is endowed with definite articles: masculine singular (*el*), feminine singular (*la*), and a plural article that does not inflect for gender (*lu*) (43).[1]

(43)
    a. El perro blanco.
         the-M.SG dog-M.SG white-M.SG
         'The white male dog.'
    b. La perra blanco.
         the-F.SG dog-F.SG white-M.SG
         'The white female dog.'
    c. Lu perro blanco.
         the-M.PL dog-M.SG white-M.SG
         'The white male dogs.'
    d. Lu perra blanco.
         the-M.PL dog-F.SG white-M.SG
         'The white female dog.'

In summary, the ABS nominal domain has the following characteristics: singular bare nouns in argument position, count/mass distinction, morphological plural, lack of a generalized classifier system, and presence of definite articles. These features make ABS a language that does not fit into Chierchia's Nominal Parameter typology. In the next section, we will take a closer look at ABS bare singular nouns in order to understand which semantic and syntactic principles regulate their properties.

5.2. Number and Mass Interpretation

ABS bare nouns appear to not be specified for number and are able to take on either a mass or a count reading (plural or singular) depending on the context in which they appear. The nature of these nouns will be exempli-

---

1. Lipski (2008: 82) hypothesized that ABS *lu* might have been the only definite article in the early stages of ABS formation. This would be suggested by the fact that *lu* is not only used as a plural article; rather, in his recordings the author could find sporadic instances in which *lu* takes on a singular reading (e.g. *lu juamía* 'the family'). I am not in the position of either confirming or rejecting this statement, since none of my informants were aware of the singular use of *lu* and my recordings do not report cases in which it acts as a singular definite article.

fied by presenting several grammatical tests, also used by Kester & Schmitt
(2007: 127–29) to illustrate similar phenomena in Brazilian Portuguese and
Papiamentu. ABS bare singulars are interpreted as plural when they are
objects of verbs imposing a non-atomicity entailment on their internal argument (44).

(44) Pedro colecciona película.
      Pedro collects movie-SG
      'Pedro collects movies.'

Ns take on a singular reading when they occur in the same position, but
with verbs that impose an atomicity entailment on their internal argument
(45).

(45) Ana quele ti casar con boliviano.
      Ana wants you marry with Bolivian-SG
      'Ana wants you to marry a Bolivian.' (any Bolivian)

Discourse anaphora provides further evidence for the systematic ambiguity between a singular and a plural reading of bare nouns. In fact, in ABS
they can be referred back to with either a plural or a singular pronoun, as
illustrated in (46).

(46) Yo tiene hijo. Ele/Eyu vive a Mururata.
      I have child-SG He/They live to Mururata
      'I have a child/children. He/They live in Mururata.'

Moving now to the mass/count distinction, ABS mass nouns may appear
bare in argument position, where they can take on either an existential reading (47a) or a generic one (47b).

(47)
      a. Agua ta fríu.
          water is cold
          'The water is cold.'
      b. Oro ta caro.
          gold is expensive.
          'Gold is expensive.'

These data indicate that bare singulars allow mass and count readings. With respect to the latter, they can be interpreted as atomic or non-atomic individuals, and they can be linked to singular or plural pronouns.

5.3. Bare Nouns as Names of Kinds

In his Ph.D. dissertation, Carlson (1977) proposed a set of semantic tests to show that in English bare plurals in argument position are interpreted as names of kinds. The same hypothesis has been adopted recently by Kester & Schmitt (2007) to account for Brazilian Portuguese and Papiamentu data. In the present section, I provide some of these tests to describe the nature of ABS bare nouns. Carlson (1977) and Kester & Schmitt (2007) illustrate their point by showing that in these languages bare plurals yield to a grammatical interpretation when they co-occur with predicates that can describe only kinds; the authors also demonstrate that the interpretation of bare nouns is sensitive to the context in which they appear, and that they cannot take wide scope over negation, intensional verbs, and durative adverbials. In this respect, ABS singular bare nouns appear to parallel bare plurals in English, Brazilian Portuguese, and Papiamentu.

Example (48) illustrates how ABS bare nouns combine with predicates that apply only to kinds.

(48) Chancho es muy común a Tocaña
      pig-SG is very common to Tocaña
      'Pigs are very common in Tocaña.'

The generic and existential readings of bare nouns are conditioned by well-known factors such as the lexical requirements of the predicate, tense/aspect, episodicity, etc. For example, the bare singular in (49) is interpreted generically, whereas the one in (50) is existential:

(49) A mí me gusta gato.
      to me to-me like cat-SG
      'I like cats.'

(50) Tiene gallina en la casa.
      have chicken-SG in the-SG house-SG
      'There is a chicken/chickens in the house.'

Finally, when co-occurring with negation (51a), intensional verbs (51b), and durative adverbials (51c), bare singulars allow only narrow-scope readings.

(51)

    a. Oté no vió mancha en la ventana. (neg > object; *object > neg)
        you no saw spot-SG in the-SG window-SG
        'You did not see the spot on the window.'

    b. Juana quele ti casar con boliviano. (want > object; *object > want)
        Juana want you marry with Bolivian-SG
        'Juana wants you to marry a Bolivian.' (any Bolivian)

    c. o mató iguana por dos hora. (adv > object; *object > adv)
        I killed iguana-SG for two hour-SG
        'I killed iguanas for two hours.'

This section has shown that ABS singular bare nouns can receive a kind reading when occurring in argument position. This is their default reading; however, such an interpretation is not the only one they have. As we will see in the following sections, depending on the pragmatic context in which they appear, these Ns can receive either a definite or an indefinite reading.

5.4. The Semantics of (In)definiteness

This section provides a description of ABS article system with respect to the semantic notions of definiteness and specificity. The article system of contact languages has generated much interest in creole linguistics, especially after Bickerton's (1981) stipulations on its nature in creole languages. According to Bickerton, creole languages are endowed with an article system with "a definite article for presupposed-specific NP; an indefinite article for asserted-specific NP; and zero for nonspecific NP" (1981: 56). As we will see in more detail, this description does not capture the features of ABS article system. In this vernacular, in fact, there are three overt definite articles (*el, la, lu*) and two indefinite ones (*un, unos*). Moreover, I claim that null articles are present, but they are not restricted to non-specific NPs. The distribution of articles in ABS resembles that of standard Spanish with the exception that bare nouns can take on plural/singular, definite/indefinite, specific/non-specific readings, given the appropriate syntactic and pragmatic environment.

5.4.1. BARE NOUNS AND INDEFINITENESS

I begin this section analyzing the distributional properties and uses of the indefinite *un/unos*. Indefinite articles in ABS can refer to both specific and non-specific entities where, from a pragmatic point of view, an entity is specific if it is known by the speaker, by the hearer, or by both (see Gutiérrez-Rexach 2004). Examples (52a, b) clarify this distinction between specific and non-specific uses. In (52a) the speaker knows which chocolate cake(s) he acquired yesterday; in (52b) he does not know exactly which cake(s) he will buy tomorrow; he knows only that he will be looking for a/some chocolate one(s).

(52)

    a.   Ayer yo compró un/unos tarta de chocolate.
        yesterday I bought a/some cake of chocolate
        'Yesterday I bought a/some chocolate cake(s).'

    b.   Mañana yo va comprar un/unos tarta de chocolate.
        tomorrow I go buy a/some cake of chocolate
        'Tomorrow I will buy a/some chocolate cake(s).'

The same specific/non-specific reading of indefinites can be taken on by the noun when it is preceded by a null determiner (53a, b).

(53)

    a.   Ayer yo compró tarta de chocolate.
        yesterday I bought cake of chocolate
        'Yesterday I bought a/some chocolate cake(s).'

    b.   Mañana yo va comprar tarta de chocolate.
        tomorrow I go buy cake of chocolate
        'Tomorrow I will buy a/some chocolate cake(s).'

The only distinction between the sentences in (52) and those in (53) is that in the first case the number (singular/plural) is conveyed by the overt determiner, while in the second set of sentences it is not. In fact, a strategy commonly used in ABS to distinguish between single and plural readings consists of recurring to indefinite articles, as illustrated below (54).

(54)   Oté tiene caramelo? Sí, yo tiene caramelo/un caramelo.
       you have candy yes I have candy/a candy
       'Do you have candies? Yes, I have candies/a candy.'

Indefinite singulars can also have wide and narrow scope with respect to other operators, such as negation and intensional verbs.

(55)

    a.   Yo no vio un mancha en el suelo. (un > ¬ and ¬ > un)
        I not see a spot on the floor
        'I didn't see a spot on the floor.'

    b.   Juana quele ti casar con un italiano. (want > un and un > want)
        Juana want you marry with un Italian
        'Juana wants you to marry an Italian.'

Moreover, indefinites in ABS can have a generic reading, which should not be confused with the kind-denoting reading. In fact, indefinites can appear with quantificational generics (56a), but cannot occur with predicates that can only be true of a kind (56b) (see also Kester & Schmitt 2007: 122–23) or with one-event-only episodic predicates (56c).

(56)

    a.   Un inglés habla inglés.
        an Englishman speaks English
        'An Englishman speaks English.'

    b.   *Un gallinazo/gallinazo ta en peligro de extinción.
        a black-buzzard/black buzzard is in danger of extinction
        'Black buzzards are on the verge of extinction.'

    c.   *Un negro/negro votó por primera vez después Reforma Agraria.
        a black/black voted for first time after reform agricultural
        'Black people voted for the first time after the Land Reform.'

Therefore, singular bare nouns can be kind-referring expressions while nouns preceded by indefinite articles cannot. Müller (2003: 78–81) showed a variety of differences and commonalities between indefinites and bare singulars in Brazilian Portuguese. A similar scenario is also true for ABS. In fact, in this contact dialect, both indefinites and bare singulars take on a generic reading when they are subjects of episodic predicates. Nevertheless, in sentences like (57), the indefinite subject can also have a specific interpretation—"A certain Bolivian eats lechón today"—while such a reading is not available for the bare noun, which is always understood as existential/

generic, when uttered out of the blue—"Bolivians in general eat *lechón* today."

(57)
    a. Un boliviano come lechón hoy.
        A Bolivian eats lechón today
        'A Bolivian eats lechón today.'
    b. Boliviano come lechón hoy.
        Bolivian eats lechón today
        'Bolivians eats lechón today.'

Moreover, in (58), a generic reading obtains for both sentences; this effect is highly dependent on the essential properties of the noun. In fact, a defining, essential property of 'being a sonnet' consists of 'having four strophes' (see Gutiérrez-Rexach 2006 for a characterization of essential properties). On the other hand, in (59a), it is not possible to ascribe to 'a romantic song' the essential property of 'being popular,' so that *un canción romántico* cannot be interpreted generically. Conversely, the construction in (59b) yields to a grammatical reading because it has a descriptive or inductive flavor (Greenberg 2003).

(58)
    a. Un soneto tiene cuatro estrofa.
        a sonnet has four strophes
        'A sonnet has four strophes.'
    b. Soneto tiene cuatro estrofa.
        sonnet has four strophes
        'Sonnets have four strophes.'

(59)
    a. #Un canción romántico es popular.
        a song romantic is popular
        'A romantic song is popular.'
    b. Canción romántico es popular.
        song romantic is popular
        'Love songs are popular.'

When an indefinite noun expresses an unusual class, it tends to receive an existential reading, whereas bare nouns of the same type tend to take on a generic interpretation. The bare nouns in (60) have a generic reading. The generic interpretation is possible not only for bare nouns denoting well-known or common classes, such as a "famous actor" in (60a); it is also available for bare nouns referring to very unusual ones, such as a "Bolivian musicians born on the fourth of August in Cochabamba" in (61a). On the other hand, both the generic and the existential interpretations are available for the indefinite noun in (61b); nevertheless, the existential specific reading is strongly favored.

(60)

    a.   Actor famoso gana mucho dinero.
           actor famous earns much money
           'Famous actors make a lot of money.'

    b.   Un actor famoso gana mucho dinero.
           an actor famous earns much money
           'A famous actor makes a lot of money'

(61)

    a.   Músico boliviano nacido el 4 de agosto en Cochabamba
           toma harto cerveza.
           musician Bolivian born the 4 of August in Cochabamba
           drinks much beer
           'Bolivian musicians born on the fourth of August in Cochabamba drink a lot of beer.'

    b.   Un músico boliviano nacido el 4 de agosto en Cochabamba
           toma harto cerveza.
           a musician Bolivian born the 4 of August in Cochabamba
           drinks much beer
           'A Bolivian musician born on the fourth of August in Cochabamba drinks much beer.'

In summary, both bare nouns and indefinites can express genericity. Indefinites express only generalizations that are backed up by information shared in the common ground, whereas bare nouns express generalizations *per se*, not triggering supporting presuppositions (Greenberg 2003). With respect to existential/indefinite readings, bare nouns have an existential reading only if uttered out of the blue; indefinites have either a generic or an existential interpretation depending on the presence or absence of triggering presuppositions. In addition, bare nouns do not indicate number information (singular/plural), while *un/unos* inherently convey this feature as a result of their morphological specification.

5.4.2. BARE NOUNS AND DEFINITENESS

ABS bare nouns can take on readings that are similar to those of DPs headed by definite determiners. Nevertheless, such interpretations are strongly dependent on the pragmatic context in which they occur. As an example, bare nouns cannot be interpreted as definite (indicating existence plus uniqueness) if uttered out of the blue—i.e., they have to satisfy a familiarity presupposition. Both definite descriptions and bare nouns can be associated to an antecedent in discourse via identity or a part-whole relation, satisfying a strong familiarity presupposition (Roberts 2003). An example of an identity relation between discourse referents is presented in (62), where the (b) sentence is a continuation of the (a) sentence (see Kester & Schmitt 2007: 117).

(62)
    a.   Yo compró un tarta.
         I bought a cake
         'I bought a cake.'
    b.   Tarta/la tarta sabe a fresa.
         cake/the cake taste like strawberry
         'The cake tastes like strawberry.'

The above example shows that bare nouns can also refer back to discourse-familiar entities, and, not being specified for number, they can be linked to singular or plural discourse referents. Both definite articles and bare nouns can also refer back to weakly familiar entities (Roberts 2003). Instances of weak familiarity are represented by the so-called bridging or associative contexts (Asher & Lascarides 1998), which may be triggered by a part-whole relation between the entities in discourse (see Kester & Schmitt 2007: 118). In (63), *crema/la crema* 'cream/the cream' is understood as the cake's cream.

(63)
    a.   Yo compró un tarta.
         I bought a cake
         'I bought a cake.'

    b.   Crema/la crema sabe a fresa.
        cream/the cream taste like strawberry
        'The cream tastes like strawberry.'

Definite determiners and bare nouns allow attributive and referential interpretations of a nominal description. They differ in that attributive readings of bare nouns are possible only when such an attribute is salient in the common ground. Example (64a) allows for two different interpretations: one in which I know the teacher and I am looking for him, and another in which I am looking for the teacher without exactly knowing who this person is. Nevertheless, (64b) can be uttered only in a scenario (common ground) in which the relevant properties or attributes are salient—for example, a school. It would not be felicitous, for example, if uttered while addressing a server in a bar, unless the teacher were a well-known regular customer.

(64)
    a.   Yo ta buscando el maestro.
        I is looking for the teacher
        'I am looking for the teacher.'
    b.   Yo ta buscando maestro.
        I is looking for teacher
        'I am looking for the teacher.'

Sometimes the use of bare nouns approximates that of demonstrative elements, in that not only the presuppositions associated with definiteness are satisfied (existence and uniqueness), but also a demonstration presupposition (Roberts 2001). The deictic content of bare nouns can also be derived by visual cues. In (65), if the mentioned entities are pointed out by the speaker, no definite or demonstrative article is required and the bare noun is understood as a demonstrative description:

(65)   Nube ta bien rojo.
       cloud be good red
       'That cloud/those clouds is/are very red.'

Definite DPs in ABS, like bare nouns, can combine with predicates of kinds (66a) and with one-event-only episodic predicates (66b):

(66)
    a. El gallinazo ta en peligro de extinción.
        the black-buzzard is on-the-verge of extinction
        'Black buzzards are on the verge of extinction.'
    b. El negro votó por primera vez después Reforma Agraria.
        the black voted for first time after Reform Land
        'Black people voted for the first time after the Land Reform.'

In summary, this section shows that bare singular nouns can alternate with definite DPs in ABS. This is possible only when the relevant presuppositions are satisfied in the common ground. Said interpretation can be made explicit through an anaphoric identity relation, part-whole relation, common-ground cues, uniqueness presuppositions, or visual deixis.

5.5. Bare Nouns in ABS: A Unified Account

In this section, I provide a theoretical account of the attested patterns. First, it seems clear that the Nominal Mapping Parameter (Chierchia 1998) does not adequately explain the ABS data. As observed, ABS does not fit into Chierchia's framework: ABS bare nouns occur in argument position, this language has plural morphology, and the count/mass distinction is instantiated at the lexical level. Following Longobardi (1994), we can assume that bare nouns are not structurally bare; rather, they are embedded into a DP, with an empty D category (see also Contreras 1986). DPs can act as arguments, while NPs are predicates; thus they need to combine with a D head to be referential. The nom (∩) operation takes place in D to shift common nouns, which denote properties <s,<e,t>>, into individuals <s,e>.

Covert determiners in ABS encode a variety of functions, not only nom. Covert type-shifting operations can be seen as last resort mechanisms that provide "bare" DPs with kind and quantificational interpretations. Such operations are not allowed if there is an overt determiner performing the same function. In ABS we see that there are definite and indefinite determiners, but bare nouns can still receive indefinite or definite-like interpretations without the presence of those items, although the resulting interpretations are not identical.

ABS bare nouns lack number specification. Number and quantificational force are encoded at the D level (Delicado-Cantero & Sessarego 2011). This particular configuration allows for a wider array of interpretive possibilities, depending on which operator is inserted. In the case of bare nouns in ABS, the evidence presented here suggests that a covert determiner may encode a variety of type-shifting functions (Partee & Rooth 1983): (i) nom: for the shift of predicates to kind readings in the default case; (ii) existential or definite (iota) operators: for existential and definite-like interpretations. In the case of the existential operator, pure existential readings are favored; for the definite readings, familiarity presuppositions have to be satisfied in the common ground. In general, ABS instantiates a very flexible system, where the absence of overt morphological marking on nouns allows for contextual parameters to determine the interpretation of bare DPs. This flexibility is required, given that not only morphological marking and semantic type determine the interpretation of the bare noun, but also contextual factors.

5.6. Conclusion

Far from postulating new revolutionary linguistic parameters, this study has shown that Chierchia's proposal cannot account for the ABS data. This chapter provided a survey and analysis of the nature of bare nouns in ABS. It also compared the properties of definite and indefinite determiners with those of bare nouns.

ABS bare nouns have been analyzed as names of kinds subject to type-shifting operations determined by contextual factors. In turn, these elements obey certain semantic and pragmatic constraints, which ultimately determine the interpretation of their covert D-categories.

6

N-Ellipsis

6.0. Introduction

This chapter is a survey of N-ellipsis phenomena in standard Spanish (stSp) and Afro-Bolivian Spanish (ABS); the examples provided here were collected through formal elicitations since spontaneous speech was unlikely to provide the grammatical accuracy required in the judgments for the analysis of the syntactic configurations under investigation.

The generative literature on Spanish N-ellipsis is particularly rich, so that different frameworks have been designed to account for the processes responsible for its distribution in the standard variety. Some scholars have indicated that Spanish richness in inflectional morphology and the presence of *pro* in this language are the reasons making N-ellipses possible (Torrego 1988); some accounts have explained the nature of Spanish N-drop by recurring to N movement to DP-internal Agreement Projections to check nominal phi-features (Kester & Sleeman 2002; Ticio 2003, 2005); others have ascribed nominal properties to the preposition *de* 'of' to explain cliticization of the article to the preposition after the ellipsis operation has taken place (Brucart 1987, 1999; Brucart & Gràcia 1986). Interestingly, a comparison between the stSp (67) and the ABS (68) data indicates that although ABS is not inflectionally rich and does not have *pro*, it allows all the elliptical configurations encountered in stSp. Moreover, ABS nouns can also be frequently elided in constructions that would be ungrammatical in stSp, namely when the elided noun is followed by *cun* 'with'.

(67) stSp
    a. La camisa roja y la [e] de manchas.
        the shirt red and the [e] of spots
    b. *La camisa roja y la [e] con manchas.
        the shirt red and the [e] with spots
        'The red shirt and the spotted one.'

(68) ABS
    a. La camisa rojo y la [e] de mancha.
        the shirt red and the [e] of spot
    b. La camisa rojo y la [e] cun mancha.
        the shirt red and the [e] with spot
        'The red shirt and the spotted one.'

All of this represents problems for previous explanations and will be addressed in the current chapter by adopting a microparametric minimalist perspective (see van Craenenbroeck 2010 for a complementary perspective).

6.1. Data

In stSp, where gender and number agreement operates across the DP, a switch in number features across clauses allows nominal elision to obtain (sloppy identity), while differences in gender specification on N block the elliptical process (Depiante & Masullo 2001; Saab 2004) (69).

(69) stSp
    a. El chico alto y los [e] bajos.
        the-M.SG boy-M.SG tall-M.SG and the-M.PL [e] short-M.PL
        'The tall boy and the short ones.'
    b. *El chico alto y la [e] baja.
        the-M.SG boy-M.SG tall-M.SG and the-F.SG. [e] short-F.SG
        'The tall boy and the short girl.'

The same exact configurations are encountered in traditional ABS, where nouns and adjectives do not inflect for gender and number.

(70) ABS
  a. El chico alto y lu [e] bajo.
     the-M.SG boy-M.SG. tall-M.SG and the-M.PL [e] short-M.SG
     'The tall boy and the short ones.'
  b. *El chico alto y la [e] bajo.
     the-M.SG boy-M.SG tall-M.SG and the-F.SG [e] short-M.SG
     'The tall boy and the short girl.'

In both languages, if a DP is headed by a demonstrative, a cardinal, or a quantifier, the empty nominal can stay by itself and does not have to be followed by any modifier (71–72). Conversely, if the D element is a definite article, [e] cannot stand by itself; rather, it has to be followed by an AP, a PP, or a CP (73–74).

(71) stSp
  a. No quiero dos gatos, quiero tres [e].
     no want two cats want three
     'I do not want two cats, I want three.'
  b. No quiero estos gatos, quiero aquellos [e].
     no want these cats want those
     'I do not want these cats, I want those.'

(72) ABS
  a. Yo no quele doh gato, yo quele treh [e].
     I no want two cats I want three
     'I do not want two cats, I want three.'
  b. Yo no quele estos gato, yo quele aquellos [e].
     I no want these cats I want those
     'I do not want these cats, I want those.'

(73) stSp
  a. El gato negro y el [e] blanco.
     the cat black and the [e] white
  b. El gato negro y el [e] de color blanco.
     the cat black and the [e] of color white
  c. El gato negro y el [e] que es de color blanco.
     the cat black and the [e] that is of color white
     'The black cat and the white one.'
  d. *El gato negro y el [e]
     the cat black and the [e]

(74) ABS
   a. El gato negro y el [e] blanco.
      the cat black and the [e] white
   b. El gato negro y el [e] di color blanco.
      the cat black and the [e] of color white
   c. El gato negro y el [e] que es di color blanco.
      the cat black and the [e] that is of color white
      'The black cat and the white one.'
   d. *El gato negro y el [e].
      the cat black and the [e]

It must be acknowledged that not all adjectives behave in the same way; while post-nominal adjectives allow nominal ellipses, pre-nominal ones block them (75–76).

(75) stSp
   a. *El verdadero amigo alto y el supuesto [e] bajo.
      the true friend tall and the supposed [e] short
      'The true tall friend and the supposed short one.'
   b. El amigo alto y el [e] bajo.
      the friend tall and the [e] short
      'The tall friend and the short one.'

(76) ABS
   a. *El verdadero amigo alto y el supuesto [e] bajo.
      the true friend tall and the supposed [e] short
      'The true tall friend and the supposed short one.'
   b. El amigo alto y el [e] bajo.
      the friend tall and the [e] short
      'The tall friend and the short one.'

It should also be pointed out that D + [e] + PP constructions (see 67b, 68b) are subject to certain grammatical constraints since not all Ps can be used in these sentences. In stSp, the only P capable of following [e] in such a configuration is *de* 'of' (77); while in ABS, N-drop can occur when the elided N is followed by *di* 'of' and *cun* 'with' (78).

(77) stSp
   a. El bocadillo de jamón y el [e] de chocolate.

the sandwich of ham and the [e] of chocolate
'The ham sandwich and the chocolate one.'

   b.   *El bocadillo con jamón y el [e] con chocolate.
      the sandwich with ham and the [e] with chocolate
      'The ham sandwich and the chocolate one.'

   c.   *El bocadillo para mí y el [e] para ti.
      the sandwich for me and the [e] for you

(78) ABS

   a.   El bocadillo di jamón y el [e] di chocolate.
      the sandwich of ham and the [e] of chocolate
      'The ham sandwich and the chocolate one.'

   b.   El bocadillo cun jamón y el [e] cun chocolate.
      the sandwich with ham and the [e] with chocolate
      'The ham sandwich and the chocolate one.'

   c.   *El bocadillo para mí y el [e] para ti.
      the sandwich for me and the [e] for you

The prepositions *de/di* in stSp and ABS can take on a variety of functions. They can introduce several phrases marked with different theta-roles: possessors (79a, 80a), agents (79b, 80b), objects (79c, 80c), as well as a variety of non-thematic PPs, which provide a description of the N they modify, e.g., color adjectives. A restriction that applies to stSp and ABS N-ellipses is the need for thematic role correspondence between the coordinated clauses (compare: 79a, b, c vs. 79d, e and 80a, b, c vs. 80d, e).

(79) stSp

   a.   El libro suyo$_{poss}$ y el [e] tuyo$_{poss.}$
      the book his and the [e] your
      'His book and yours.'

   b.   El libro de Cervantes$_{agent}$ y el [e] de Juan$_{agent.}$
      the book of Cervantes and the [e] of Juan
      'Cervantes' book and Juan's one.'

   c.   El libro de física$_{object}$ y el [e] de sintaxis$_{object.}$
      the book of physics and the [e] of syntax
      'The physics book and syntax one'

   d.   *El libro de María$_{agent/poss}$ y el [e] de física$_{theme.}$
      the book of María and the [e] of physics
      'María's book and the physics one.'

e. *El libro de fisica$_{object}$ y el [e] de María$_{agent/poss.}$
the book of physics and the [e] of María
'The physics book and María's one.'

(80) ABS

a. El libro suyo$_{poss}$ y el [e] tuyo$_{poss.}$
the book his and the [e] your
'His book and your book.'

b. El libro di Cervantes$_{agent}$ y el [e] di Juan$_{agent.}$
the book of Cervantes and the [e] of Juan
'Cervantes' book and Juan's one.'

c. El libro di física$_{object}$ y el [e] di sintaxis$_{object.}$
the book of physics and the [e] of syntax
'The physics book and syntax one.'

d. *El libro di María$_{agent/poss}$ y el [e] di física$_{theme.}$
The book of María and the[e] of physics
'María's book and the physics one.'

e. *El libro di fisica$_{object}$ y el [e] di María$_{agent/poss.}$
the book of physics and the [e] of María
'The physics book and María's one.'

While theta-marked PPs must obey the thematic restrictions on coordination as exemplified in (79–80), PPs free from theta-assignment behave more freely (81).[1]

(81) stSp/ABS

a. Dame el libro de/di Juan$_{agent/poss}$ y el [e] de/di color rojo.
give-me the book of Juan and the [e] of color red
'Give me Juan's book and the red one.'

---

1. As it is well known in the literature, different arrays of theta-roles have been proposed (Belletti & Rizzi 1988; Grimshaw 1990; Jackendorff 1990; Speas 1990; etc.). Dowty (1991) suggests that we should probably focus more on the prototypicality of theta-roles, rather than enumerate the potentially endless lists of them. This idea may very well also apply in this case. However, for the sake of simplicity and conformity, here we will provide an account that considers the nominal theta-roles that have usually been treated in the literature on nominalization—namely, possessor, agent, and object (Giorgi & Longobardi 1991; Valois 1991; among others). Grammaticality judgments may vary when certain APs and de-PP constructions (potentially thematic) are introduced into the picture. However, the main point here is that there is a clear structural distinction between thematic-PPs/APs and non-thematic-ones. Thematic coordination between nominal arguments has also been pointed out by Brucart & Gràcia (1986: 9 n. 9); however, the authors did not develop a theory to account for it.

    b.   Dame el libro de/di Petrarca$_{agent}$ y el [e] de/di color rojo.
        give-me the book of Petrarca and the [e] of color red
        'Give me Petrarca's book and the red one.'

    c.   Dame el libro de/di física$_{theme}$ y el [e] de/di color rojo.
        give-me the book of physics and the [e] of color red
        'Give me the physics book and the red one.'

Finally, only CPs introduced by *que* ('that') are licit relative clause remnants; other Cs result in ungrammatical constructions (82).

(82) stSp/ABS
    a.   El boliche que es caro y el [e] que es barato.
        the shop that is expensive and the [e] that is cheap
        'The shop that is expensive and the one that is cheap.'

    b.   *El boliche donde ella compra pan y el [e] donde ella compra vino.
        the shop where she buy bread and the [e] where she buy wine
        'The shop where she buys bread and the one where she buys wine.'

This section has shown that N-drop phenomena in ABS parallel, for the most part, the instances of nominal ellipsis encountered in stSp. The only exception to this rule is the case of constructions consisting of a definite article plus [e] followed by a PP headed by *cun* 'with.' In fact, while in stSp an ellipsis followed by a *con*-PP yields an ungrammatical construction, in ABS *cun*-PP allows N-drop to obtain. While stSp and ABS converge quite closely in several aspects of their grammar (see Lipski 2008; Sessarego 2011 for an account), one aspect of these languages that is significantly divergent is the use of prepositions. The following section will briefly summarize the main differences between stSp and ABS in this respect.

6.2. Preposition Uses in ABS and stSp

Prepositions in ABS are used in ways that significantly deviate from their use in stSp. In fact, as Lipski (2008: chap. 5) points out, they are often omitted in the traditional dialect (83–86).

(83)

    a.   ABS: Nació Mururata.

        was-born Mururata

    b.   stSp: Nació en Mururata.

        was-born in Mururata

        'She was born in Mururata.'

(84)

    a.   ABS: Aprendió tomá.

        learned drink

    b.   stSp: Aprendió a tomar.

        learned to drink

        'She learned how to drink.'

(85)

    a.   ABS: Yo lleva Coroico també.

        I bring Coroico too

    b.   stSp: Yo lo llevo de Coroico también.

        I it bring of Coroico too

        'I brought this from Coroico too.'

(86)

    a.   ABS: Eyu salía mí avisá.

        they exited me tell

    b.   stSp: Ellos salían para avisarme.

        they exited for tell-me

        'They went out to let me know.'

Moreover, ABS *a* 'to' is often used as stSp *en* 'in,' with a locative function (87–89).[2]

---

2. By comparing cases like (83) and (87) we can observe that the locative preposition *a* is used variably. When faced with grammaticality judgments on the presence/absence of this element, the majority of the ABS speakers I interviewed indicated that lack of *a* has to do with a performance error, likely due to rapid speech. Nevertheless, such an intuition was not shared by everyone. Some speakers, in fact, indicated that constructions lacking *a* sounded perfectly grammatical to them, thus suggesting that, similarly to gender agreement (see chapter 7), different informants might have slightly different grammatical configurations, and variation is widespread in the community. More research is definitely needed to get a better understanding of the aforementioned phenomena.

(87)

    a.   ABS: Mi hijo vive a Mururata.
           my son live to Mururata
    b.   stSp: Mi hijo vive en Mururata.
           my son live in Mururata
           'My son lives in Mururata.'

(88)

    a.   ABS: Juan nació a La Paz.
           Juan was-born to La Paz
    b.   stSp: Juan nació en La Paz.
           Juan was-born in La Paz
           'Juan was born in La Paz.'

(89)

    a.   ABS: Mis hijo vive a la Argentina.
           my son live to the Argentina
    b.   stSp: Mis hijos viven en Argentina.
           my son live in Argentina
           'My sons live in Argentina.'

Also, *cun* is used in different ways. It can replace stSp *y* 'and' (90–92) (see Lipski 2008: 132).

(90)

    a.   ABS: Naranja cun cajué.
           orange with coffee
    b.   stSp: Naranjas y café.
           orange and coffee
           'Oranges and coffee.'

(91)

    a.   ABS: Mi tatá cun mi mamá nació Mururata.
           my dad with my mom was-born Mururata
    b.   stSp: Mi papá y mi mamá nacieron en Mururata.
           my dad and my mom were-born in Mururata
           'My father and my mother were born in Mururata.'

(92)

    a.   ABS: Mururata cun Chijchipa, nojotro siempre fue uno nomá.

          Mururata with Chijchipa we always was one no more

    b.   stSp: Mururata y Chijchipa, nosotros siempre fuimos uno no más.

          Mururata and Chijchipa we always were one no more

          'Mururata and Chijchipa, we have always been a single thing.'

Most interestingly, ABS *cun* is used in many instances in which *de* would be the preferred preposition in stSp (93–97).

(93)

    a.   ABS: Wawa cun eje edad pesa 20 kilo.

          kid with this age weight 20 kilo

    b.   stSp: Un niño de esta edad pesa 20 kilos.

          a kid of this age weight 20 kilos

          'A kid of this age weights 20 kilos.'

(94)

    a.   ABS: El hombre cun cabeza blanco.

          the man with head white

    b.   stSp: El hombre de pelo blanco.

          the man of hair white

          'The white-hair man.'

(95)

    a.   ABS: Yo ta cun pelo blanco.

          I is with hair white

    b.   stSp: Yo soy de pelo blanco / Yo tengo pelo blanco.

          I am of hair white / I have hair white

          'I have white hair.'

(96)

    a.   ABS: Eyu ta cun treinta año.

          they is with thirdy year

    b.   stSp: Ellos son de treinta años / Ellos tienen treinta años.

          they are of thirty years / They have thirty years

          'They are thirty years old.'

(97)

    a.   ABS: Eyu ta cun la cabeza bien grande.
          they is with the head well big
    b.   stSp: Ellos tienen la cabeza bien grande.
          they have the head well big
          'They have a very big head.'

In summary, there are several differences in the use of prepositions in ABS and stSp. An interesting peculiarity of ABS, which might explain why *cun*-PP can licitly survive nominal ellipsis in this vernacular, is that *cun* is often used where *de* would be preferred in stSp. As all elliptical patterns are the same in ABS and stSp with the exception of *cun/con* constructions, it may be the case that this contrast has to do with the nature of such a preposition. This statement is justified as *con/cun* presents different grammatical behaviors in the two languages. In the next section, I will describe some of the main analyses that have been proposed to account for the data in stSp.

6.3. Previous Analyses

This section will provide an overview of the main proposals concerning Spanish N-drop. These models and their predictions will be assessed with respect to the data presented in the previous section.

6.3.1. BRUCART & GRÀCIA (1986)

Brucart & Gràcia (1986) provide an analysis of ellipsis phenomena in Italian and Spanish and postulate the existence of empty N, [e], in both languages, even though parametric differences do not allow for the same exact constructions in these two Romance varieties.

In regard to Spanish, the authors argue that definite articles cannot survive ellipsis operations unless they cliticize to [+N] elements (adjectives and nouns). This would be possible with *de*-PPs, since *de* is a dummy preposition, but not with other PPs (98–99).

(98) stSp

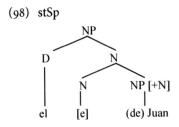

(99) stSp

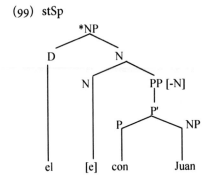

In their view, also *que* 'that' would carry [+N] features so that (100) is a licit structure, where F stands for an intermediate functional projection within DP.

(100) stSp

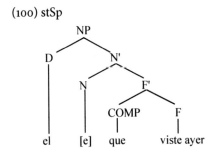

'The one that you saw yesterday'

The fact that intervening adverbials do not affect the grammaticality of these constructions can be explained in two alternative ways. First, adverbials could be seen as 'logic operators' (Guéron 1981), and, for this reason, they would be 'transparent' to cliticization processes (Brucart & Gràcia 1986: 19). Second, the article could cliticize on any element (including adverbials) if the first maximal category dominating such element is a category containing a [+N] feature in its head. An example would be (101) where *il* 'the' cliticizes on the adverbial *più* 'more,' in the SPEC of an AP preceding the noun.

(101) Italian

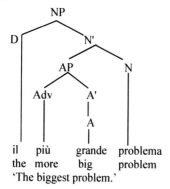

il   più   grande problema
the more   big   problem
'The biggest problem.'

    Brucart & Gràcia's (1986) account is valuable in that it recognizes the existence of empty Ns as heads of noun phrases. Nevertheless, it presents some drawbacks: it does not acknowledge the contrast in grammaticality due to variation in gender and number features, it does not provide an account for thematic correspondences between pronounced and elided Ns, and the differences between prenominal and postnominal adjectives are not addressed.

6.3.2. BRUCART (1987)

Brucart (1987: 221) presents the cases in which empty nouns are grammatical and the instances in which they are not: he provides grammatical examples (102) in which the definite article is followed by an AP (102a), a *de*-PP (102b), or a CP (102c), and ungrammatical constructions (103), lacking an overt determiner (103a), a remnant complement (103b), or presenting a PP complement headed by a preposition other than *de* (103c).

(102)

    a.   Mi cuñado utiliza el coche antiguo para ir a trabajar y el [e] nuevo para trasladarse los fines de semana a su casa de campo.

'My brother-in-law uses the old car to go to work and the new one to go to his country house during the weekend.'

b. El hijo de Luis y el [e] de Antonio se han hecho muy amigos.
   'Luis's son and Antonio's became good friends.'

c. La casa que visitaste ayer y la [e] que has visto esta mañana pertenecieron a un mismo dueño.
   'The house that you visited yesterday and the one that you have visited this morning used to belong to the same owner.'

(103)

a. *El hijo de Luis y [e] se han hecho muy amigos.
   'Luis's son and Antonio's became good friends.'

b. *El hijo de Luis y el [e] se han hecho muy amigos.
   'Luis's son and Antonio's became good friends.'

c. *El tren a Barcelona y el [e] a Madrid ha salido con retraso.
   'The train for Barcelona and the one for Madrid left late.'

Brucart argues that the examples in (102) should be classified as constructions containing an empty N, rather than as structures in which the definite articles behave as pronouns (contra Bello 1847). In fact, these articles are unstressed—as the rest of the Spanish definite articles. On the other hand, all pronouns bearing nominative case are stressed; for this reason, considering these elements as pronouns would also imply doubling the number of personal pronouns, a solution highly non-economical and counterintuitive (Brucart 1987: 225; 1999: 2856). Brucart also disagrees with other approaches that fail to identify an empty N as the nucleus of the aforementioned nominal constructions. For example, Alarcos-Llorach (1973) indicates that, in cases like (104), the nucleus would be the element following the definite article. Brucart disagrees with such an analysis since it violates the principles of X'-Theory. X'-Theory, in fact, states that projections and nuclei must belong to the same category. Nevertheless, as we can observe, in (104) what follows the definite article is neither a N nor a nominal projection, but rather a PP (Brucart 1987: 227–228).

(104) El de filosofía.
      'The one of philosophy.'

Brucart considers (104) and similar cases as instances of empty nouns acting as nominal nuclei. Such elements are not bound and should be interpreted as pronominal anaphoras PRO. In this way, it is possible to explain why a pronominal element can be understood as a previously mentioned NP. This would also explain why the empty category, if not preceded by another NP, takes on an arbitrary reading (see 105), in line with Control Theory (Chomsky 1981).

(105) El PRO que quiera asistir al concierto deberá pagar la entrada con diez días de antelación.
'The one who is interested in attending the concert will have to pay ten days in advance.'

In Brucart's view, one of the crucial components of these constructions is the presence of an overt determiner preceding the empty N; this follows from the principle of recoverability. In fact, the adoption of an overt D forces the interpretation of the remnants as complements of the elided N; on the other hand, the lack of such a restriction in natural languages could allow the interpretation of similar APs, PPs, and CPs as modifiers of other maximal projections, thus not leading to a clear and univocal reading (Brucart 1987: 231). It follows from X'-theory that the nucleus must always be present in the structure, while its complements and determiners can be optional. However, if the nucleus is an empty element, its semantic content can be recovered only if the non-nuclear categories are pronounced. For this reason, the presence of an overt D element is required (Brucart 1987: 232). Such a requirement is also related to D's referential feature and therefore to its capability of turning NPs into arguments.

The author indicates that the presence of an obligatory complement in phrases containing definite articles seems to be due to superficial factors. In fact, definite articles are clitic elements that need a host to avoid the generation of unstressed phrases. Brucart (1987: 245) attributes the grammaticality of *de*-PP remnants and the ungrammaticality of other PPs to the fact that *de* is not a 'true' preposition. As suggested for English *of* (Chomsky 1981), *de* would be inserted at PF. Differently from 'true' prepositions, *de* 'of' would simply act as a case marker and would not play a role in theta-role assignment.

Brucart (1987: 245) also points out that because of their unstressed nature, definite articles differ from other determiners in that they are the only category requiring a following complement in elliptical constructions (106).

(106)

    a.   *Buscaba el [e].
        sought the

    b.   Buscaba uno [e].
        sought a
        'I was seeking one.'

    c.   Buscaba éste [e].
        sought this
        'I was looking for this.'

    d.   Buscaba alguno [e].
        sought some
        'I was seeking some.'

    e.   Buscaba tres [e].
        sought three
        'I was looking for three.'

He also indicates that definite articles do not accept PPs different from *de*-PPs, while other determiners do (107–108).

(107) Compré el/éste/alguno/uno/tres [e] de matemáticas.
      bought the/ this/ some/one/three [e] of mathematics
      'I bought the/ this/ some/one/three of mathematics.'

(108) Compré *el/éste/alguno/uno/tres [e] con lazo.
      bought the/ this/ some/one/three [e] with lace
      'I bought the/ this/ some/one/three with lace.'

The grammaticality of all constructions in (107–108), in contrast with the ungrammaticality of the structure with *el* 'the' in (108), would be due to the fact that all the determiners but the definite articles allow the recovery of their antecedent, so that they enable PRO to participate in the assignment of thematic roles across 'true' (*con*) and 'false' (*de*) prepositions. On the other hand, the definite article does not trigger such an operation and the following constituent would be able to receive thematic assignment only if preceded by a 'false' preposition like *de* (Brucart 1987: 245).

Brucart (1987) builds on Brucart & Gràcia (1986) and provides a more detailed account of Spanish N-drop. However, it does not solve the issues left unaccounted for in the previous paper: the status of gender and number features in DP, pre/post nominal adjective contrast, and theta-role correspondences between clauses.

6.3.3. KESTER & SLEEMAN (2002)

Kester & Sleeman (2002) elaborate on Torrego's (1988) proposal, which claimed that demonstratives and quantifiers are rich enough in phi-features (gender, number, person features) to license an empty N, while definite articles must co-occur with a modifier following [e] because they are semantically weak and they lack person features, which have to be supplied by the remnant element. The modifiers allowed in this specific configuration are APs, *que*-CPs and *de*-PPs, all of which would be classified by Torrego as [+N] categories. After summarizing Torrego's generalization as (109), Kester & Sleeman (2002) provide a novel account for stSp N-drop by recurring to Kayne's (1994) Antisymmetry framework.

(109) Torrego's (1988) generalization
N-ellipsis in Spanish is licensed by the definite article when supplied with person features by a [+N] category: a *de*-modifier, a *que*-relative clause, or an adjective.

Kester & Sleeman follow Torrego's intuition that the definite article is a weak element, which must co-occur with a modifier; however, they do not agree with the generalization in (109). In fact, they suggest that the Spanish definite article is a weaker element in a semantic sense, not because of the lack of person features, but rather because it cannot be interpreted in isolation in its D° position; in fact, in order to yield a semantically interpretable construction, it has to co-occur with a predicate (Kester & Sleeman 2002: 111).

Kester and Sleeman suggest that the empty N should be analyzed as part of a CP acting as the complement of the definite article. The authors claim that "within this clausal constituent the null noun has to enter in a checking relation, at some point of the derivation, with the highest overt functional head in order to be licensed" (2002: 116). They represent the grammatical remnants stated in (109) as the structures in (110), and contrast them with examples like (111), where N-drop does not obtain.

(110)
a.   el [D/PP pro$_i$ [D/P° de [IP Juan [I [e]$_i$ ...]]]]
b.   el [CP pro$_i$ [C° que [IP nos regaló [e]$_i$ tu padre]]]
c.   la [CP pro$_i$ [C° [IP [e$_i$] [I° [amarilla]]]]]

(111) *el [CP [pro$_i$] [C° [IP [e$_i$] [I° [PP e$_i$ para Jaime]]]]]

By applying Kayne's (1994) Antisymmetry framework to the Spanish data, Kester and Sleeman state that the definite article has a clausal complement corresponding to either CP or D/PP (see 110); in this way, the empty N moves to the specifier position of such a clause and instantiates a Spec-Head relation. In (110a) and (111) the PP is analyzed as the predicate of a reduced relative clause. Pro is base-generated in SPEC-PP and moves to SPEC-CP. The reason why (110a) is grammatical while (111) is not comes from the fact that *de* 'of' is analyzed as a prepositional complementizer and, therefore, as a functional head, while *para* 'for' is analyzed as a lexical head. Since checking occurs in functional projections only (Chomsky 1995), *de* can enter in a Spec-head relation with pro, while *para* cannot. Kester and Sleeman apply the same analysis to the case of *que* 'that' (110b), which contrasts in grammaticality with other complementizers. The authors proceed also to explain cases like (110c). Indeed, they claim that the Spec-Head checking in this case is possible because pro would enter in a relation with a functional head, namely the one contained in the functional projection AgreementAP. In their view, by applying Chomsky's (1995) analysis of adjectival agreement (see 112), it is possible to reformulate (110c) as (113), where the adjective would be analyzed as the predicate of a reduced relative clause, which is contained in the functional projection AgrAP.

(112) John$_i$ is [AgrAP e$_i$ [AgrA intelligent$_j$ [AP e$_i$ e$_j$]]]

(113) la [CP pro$_i$ [IP e$_i$ [AgrAP e$_i$ [AgrA amarilla$_j$ [AP e$_i$ e$_j$]]]]]

Kester and Sleeman's analysis provides an interesting hypothesis for N-drop in stSp. The authors, in fact, are able to account for the differences in grammaticality between DPs headed by definite articles and other determiners by applying Kayne's (1994) Antisymmetry framework; nevertheless, their model leaves several issues unresolved. First of all, this account does not take in consideration the theta-marking constraints exemplified in examples (79–80). Secondly, the postulation of an AgrP, to which N should move, appears counterintuitive since we know that sloppy identity across clauses is allowed for number but not for gender, thus suggesting that these two features should not be checked in the same syntactic position. Finally, also in this case, there is no mention of the ungrammaticality of N-drop with prenominal As.

6.3.4. TICIO (2003, 2005)

In line with Grohmann & Haegeman (2002), Ticio (2003, 2005) assumes a DP-internal structure subdivided into three prolific domains: a domain in which theta-roles are assigned; a domain devoted to phi-agreement and case relations; and a domain in which discourse information is encoded. Ticio also proposes different positions for adjectives according to their semantic properties: prenominal As would be located in SPEC-NP, postnominal As are adjoined to NP, and R(elational) As are generated in SPEC-nP.

(114)

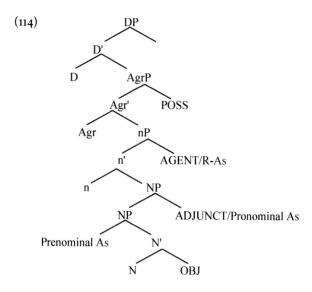

Ticio accounts for the ungrammaticality of pronominal adjectives in elliptical construction by suggesting that the ellipsis operation targets only the lower NP node, and therefore, it does not affect the adjectives generated in higher projections (see 115; see Ticio 2005: 136).

(115)   (. . .)

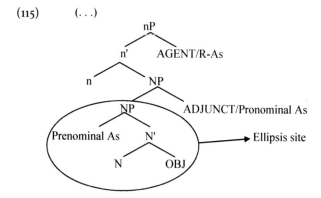

Ticio (2005: 136–137) provides examples to show how this model accounts for Adjuncts (116a), Postnominal As (116b), Possessors (116c), Agents (116d), R-As (116e), and Prenominal As (116f); however, she admits that—at first glance—her proposal does not explain why Objects can survive ellipses (116g) even though they should not since they are base-generated in a position lower than the NP-node.

(116) stSp

    a.   Compramos bastantes libros para regalo y uno [e]
        [para consulta]$_{adjunct.}$
        (we)bought several books to gift and a [e] to consult
        'We bought several books as gifts and one for our records.'

    b.   Compramos varios libros azules y uno [e] rojo.
        (we)bought several books blue and a [e] red
        'We bought several blue books and red one.'

    c.   Compramos varios libros de Luis y uno [e] [de María]$_{poss.}$
        (we)bought several books of Luis and a [e] of María
        'We bought several blue books of Luis' and one of María's.'

    d.   Compramos varios libros de Cervantes y uno [e]
        [de Borges]$_{ag.}$
        (we)bought several books of Cervantes and a [e] of Borges
        'We bought several blue books of Cervantes' and one of Borges."

    e.   Compramos varias novelas policíacas y una [e] romántica.
        (we)bought several novels police and a [e] romantic
        'We bought several police novels and a romantic one.'

    f.   *Ayer vi a la verdadera terrorista y a la supuesta [e].
        yesterday (I)saw to the true terrorist and to the alleged [e]
        'Yesterday, I saw the true terrorist and the alleged one.'

    g.   Compramos varios libros de Matemáticas y alguno [e]
        [de Física]$_{obj.}$
        (we)bought several books of Math and some [e] of Physics
        'We bought several Math books and a Physics one.'

In order to solve this problem, Ticio proposes that a stylistic rule would be able to move the object from its original site to a higher position in the syntactic tree before the ellipsis operation applies, as shown in (117).

(117) stSp

Varios [e] de Física_obj de Juan_poss.

several [e] of Physics of Juan

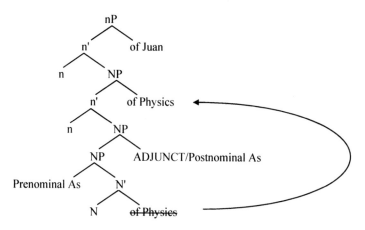

Finally, she provides an account for why, in the presence of definite articles, no other PPs can be found as remnants except those headed by *de*. In line with Brucart & Gràcia (1986) and Raposo (1999), Ticio highlights the clitic-like character of definite articles, which seem to be able to cliticize only on [+N] elements (adjectives and nouns). Ticio also assumes that cliticization processes cannot take place across phase boundaries since phases are conceived as spell-out units. In her view, two different types of PPs are found in Spanish: full PPs (which constitute phases), headed by Ps like *con* 'with,' and 'false' PPs (which do not constitute phases), headed by *de* 'of' (2005: 140). This would explain the ungrammaticality of (118) and the grammaticality of (119). In fact, in (118) the presence of *con* gives rise to a phase boundary at Spell-Out, which prevents article cliticization; on the other hand, in (119), the article can freely cliticize, since *de* is inserted after Spell-Out and does not introduce a new phase unit.

(118) stSp
   a.   [DP La [[NP chica] || [PP con gafas]]] Spell Out
   b.   [DP La [[NP e]] || [PP con gafas]]] NP-Ellipsis
   c.   *[DP La [[NP e]] || [PP con gafas]]] Cliticization

(119) stSp
    a.   [DP La [[NP chica] [NP gafas]]] Spell Out
    b.   [DP La [[NP e] [NP gafas]]] NP-ellipsis
    c.   [DP La [[NP e] DE-[NP gafas]]] DE(of)-insertion
    d.   [DP La [[NP e] + DE-[NP gafas]]] Cliticization

This account also presents some drawbacks. First, the postulation of pre-nominal and post-nominal adjective base-generated positions is somehow problematic in that it goes against hypotheses assuming that all adjectives are originally pre-nominal and the overt distribution is just a result of N movement (Cinque 1990, 1993, 2004, 2005, 2007). Second, the postulation of an Agreement Projection in which all phi-features are checked cannot capture the grammaticality distinctions pointed out in (120–121), where number but not gender can survive to NP-ellipses. Moreover, it also goes against recent hypotheses arguing in favor of the elimination of Agreement Projections (Chomsky 2002).

(120) stSp
    a.   Los gatos negros y el [e] blanco.
        the-M.PL cat-M.PL black-M.PL and the-M.SG [e] white-M.SG
        'The black cats and the white one.'
    b.   *El gato negro y la [e] blanca.
        the-M.SG cat-M.SG black-M.SG and the-F.SG [e] white-F.PL
        'The black cat and the white one.'

(121) ABS
    a.   Lu gato negro y el [e] blanco.
        the-M.PL cat-M.PL black-M.PL and the-M.SG [e] white-M.SG
        'The black cats and the white one.'
    b.   *El gato negro y la [e] blanca.
        the-M.SG cat-M.SG black-M.SG and the-F.SG [e] white-F.PL
        'The black cat and the white one.'

Third, postulating that articles can cliticize only to [+N] elements does not explain why examples like (122, 123) are grammatical.

(122) stSp
    a.   El chico italiano y el [e] supuestamente italiano.
        the guy Italian and the [e] supposedly Italian
        'The Italian guy and the supposedly Italian one.'

b. Los chicos de Italia y los [e] supuestamente de Italia.
   the guys of Italy and the [e] supposedly of Italy
   'The Italian guys and the supposedly Italian ones.'

(123) ABS
   a. El chico italiano y el [e] supuestamente italiano.
      the guy Italian and the [e] supposedly Italian
      'The Italian guy and the supposedly Italian one.'
   b. Lu chico di Italia y lu [e] supuestamente di Italia.
      The guys of Italy and the [e] supposedly of Italy
      'The Italian guys and the supposedly Italian ones.'

Examples such as (118, 119) clearly show that APs and PPs modified by adverbs [–N] are actually licit remnants. In order to account for these constructions, we should postulate that adverbs are inserted later in the derivation, after ellipsis applies, like *de*. This hypothesis does not seem feasible. Moreover, movement of objects before ellipsis and *de* insertion at PF seems to be a somewhat ad hoc solution rather that a theoretically motivated operation since it is not clear why objects would be targeted in such a fashion and not subjects or adjuncts. In addition, Ticio (2005) does not provide an account for the differences between relative clauses headed by *que* and those headed by other relativizers. Finally, this analysis assumes a right-branching structure with right-sided specifiers and rightward movement operations. Such syntactic machinery goes against standard assumptions on left branching and dislocation, and it would also violate the Linear Correspondence Axiom (see Kayne 1994).

6.4. Toward a New Proposal

This section provides a new model to explain the data so far presented. The proposal is based on several assumptions concerning the structure of DP, which account for the grammatical and ungrammatical cases of N-ellipsis. It does not recur to ad hoc insertion operations or constituent movement. It rather bases the observed differences on pure structural distinctions.

The difference between definite articles and the rest of the determiners is based on semantic principles. My proposal assumes that certain determiners (demonstratives,[3] etc.) are encoded with a [+referential] feature, indicating

---

3. Even though they are context-dependent, demonstratives in Spanish may refer un-

referential independence. In other words, from a semantic standpoint, the definite article is a restricted element (Higginbotham 1985). Indeed, it must co-occur with an overt predicate, since it cannot be interpreted alone in its D° position (see Chierchia 1998; Kester & Sleeman 2002). The co-occurrence of the article with such a predicate (e.g., [e] + overt remnant) leads to a semantically interpretable object (to phase completion).

Syntactically, when demonstratives, cardinals, etc. are base-generated under their respective projections or possibly moved to SPEC-DP to check their referential feature, they essentially freeze the DP as it is (see Cardinaletti & Giusti 1991; Gutiérrez-Rodríguez 2009; Ishane 2008; Zamparelli 2000 for a treatment of base-generation and movements of these elements within the DP). The DP then acts as a pronoun-like element regardless of the existence of an overt N.[4] This accounts for the following examples (124, 125).

(124) ABS
    a.   Ejes chica di Italia y aquellos [e].
        these girls of Italy and those [e]
        'These Italian girls and those.'
    b.   *Lu chica di Italia y lu [e].
        the girls of Italy and the [e]

(125) stSp
    a.   Estas chicas de Italia y aquellas [e].
        these girls of Italy and those [e]
        'These Italian girls and those.'
    b.   *Las chicas de Italia y las [e].
        The girls of Italy and the [e]

Additionally, my analysis, as Ticio's, takes into consideration the well-known existence of thematic layers in the DP, which have been shown to hold across several languages with respect to certain phenomena such as blocking effects in extraction.[5] I assume the nominal theta-role hierarchy suggested in Giorgi & Longobardi (1991) and Valois (1991) among others (126).[6]

---

equivocally to a previous discourse item. They pattern like proper names in this sense, and therefore need not occur with a noun (e.g., demonstrative pronouns).
    4. See Leonetti (1990) for a more detailed account of this issue.
    5. For a detailed account, see Giorgi & Longobardi (1991) for Italian, Valois (1991) for French, and Ticio (2003) for Spanish.
    6. I also acknowledge that much research has been done on theta-roles, many hypotheses

(126) Possessor>>Agent>>Object

I propose an account in which *de* 'of' is treated as a complementizer head without N features, in line with Kayne (1994). I consider stSp *de* and ABS *di* multifunctional prepositions. They not only have the capability of heading argumental PPs; additionally, *de/di* structures are the syntactic result of commonly used strategies to create adjective-like modifiers for nouns (den Dikken 2003). I argue that all adjectives are base-generated pre-nominally (Cinque 1993, 2005, 2007), merge to the left of NP, and are always phrasal (Bosque & Picallo 1996; Picallo 2010). Ellipses affect only the lower DP-internal layer, targeting N. This explains why cases of sloppy identity for number are allowed, while the same cannot occur with gender:

(127) stSp
    a.   Los gatos negros y el [e] blanco.
        the-M.PL cat-M.PL black-M.PL. and the-M.SG [e] white-M.SG
        'The black cats and the white one.'
    b.   *El gato negro y la [e] blanca
        the-M.SG. cat-M.SG black-M.SG and the-F.SG [e] white-F.SG

In fact, gender is analyzed here as an interpretable feature of N. Number interpretation is located in Num, in a higher projection, where it survives N-ellipsis (Depiante & Masullo 2001; Saab 2004). This account, therefore, does not postulate specific Agreement Projections to which N must move (contra Kester & Sleeman 2002; Ticio 2003, 2005) and is in line with the minimalist proposal to eliminate Agreement Projections (Chomsky 2002). Even though ABS does not present redundant number and gender agreement across DP, the constructions in (128) show a clear parallelism between ABS and stSp.

(128) ABS
    a.   Lu gato negro y el [e] blanco.
        the-M.PL cat-M.SG black-M.SG and the-M.SG [e] white-M.SG
        'The black cats and the white one.'
    b.   *El gato negro y la [e] blanco
        the-M.SG cat-M.SG black-M.SG and the-F.SG [e] white-M.SG

have been made, but the precise nature of these thematic relations is still not completely clear. See Dowty (1991) for a more detailed account.

In ABS, as well as in stSp, gender, differently from number, is a feature of the noun, which gets deleted in the process of ellipsis. This fact strongly undermines approaches postulating a unique projection for number and gender (e.g., Ritter 1991, 1993), and partially those that argue in favor of two separate projections NumP and a GenP as well (e.g., Picallo 1991; Bernstein 1993). In fact, masculine and feminine nouns in ABS do not seem to be derivable from the same lexical entry. Data support a framework in which lexical entries are clearly different in gender specification before entering the syntactic numeration. Therefore, only NumP is a licit projection, while 'gender' represents an interpretable feature of N.

In line with Carstens (2000), I assume that thematic roles are assigned under nP. Adjectives and *de*-phrases carrying Θ-assignment are initially merged within the nP shells. Other adjectives and *de*-phrases free from Θ-assignment (i.e., *La camisa roja* 'the red shirt', *La camisa de color rojo* 'the shirt of red color') are merged higher in the structure, and, for this reason, they are able to survive universal ellipsis operations (Merchant 2001). A strict correspondence between the thematic roles of the parallel constituents (Lobeck 1995) is required in both varieties (129).

(129) stSp/ABS
   a. El libro de/di física$_{theme}$ y el [e] de/di historia$_{theme.}$
      the book of physics and the [e] of history
      'The physics book and his one.'
   b. *El libro de/di física$_{theme}$ y el [e] de/di María$_{poss.}$
      the book of physics and the [e] of María
      'The physics book and María's.'

This suggests that the thematic properties under nP are spelled out in the nominal phase requiring both thematic configurations to match. Differences in grammaticality between ABS and stSp are reduced to elliptical constructions involving the preposition *cun* 'with', which in ABS shows striking similarities to stSp *de* in a variety of contexts (130–131).

(130) ABS
   a. El hombre cun pelo blanco toma agua.
      the man with hair white drink water
      'The white-hair man drinks water.'
   b. Wawa cun eje edad pesa veinte kilo.
      kid with this age weight twenty kilo
      'A kid of this age weighs twenty kilos.'

(131) stSp
a. El hombre de pelo blanco toma agua.
the man of hair white drink water
'The white-hair man drinks water.'
b. Un niño de esta edad pesa veinte kilos.
a kid of this age weight twenty kilos
'A kid of this age weighs twenty kilos.'

The fact that a strict correspondence between thematic roles is required between the pronounced and the elided constituents suggests that the information generated under nP gets frozen. The speaker expects it to match with the thematic configuration of the elided N. For this reason, I postulate that As and PPs—when free from any potential theta-role assignment—are generated higher in the structure, in a projection different from the one stipulated for the rest of post-nominal non-thematic adjectives.

Note that the present proposal does not need to stipulate ad hoc object movements or procrastinated *de* insertion at PF (Ticio 2003, 2005); nor does it need to assign special [+N] features to *de* and *que* (see Torrego 1988). The syntactic process involved in N-ellipsis seems to be capable of recovering only the N information, freezing the structure projected from the lower thematic nP (object) up to the higher nP (possessor) Such a process allows variability for the information contained in higher projections (NumP, non-thematic-APs/de-PPs).

To account for the differences in grammaticality between stSp *con* and ABS *cun*, I propose that *cun* in ABS shares structural properties with stSp *de* as suggested by cross-linguistic data; in fact, as we noticed in section 6.2, prepositions are used differently in the two varieties, and ABS *cun* appears in many contexts in which in stSp *de* would be employed rather than *con*. As a consequence, constructions like (132) in stSp are ungrammatical while cases like (133) in ABS allow N-drop.

(132) stSp
*... y la [e] con gafas
... and the [e] with glasses
'... the one with glasses'

(133) ABS
... y la [e] cun gafa
... and the [e] with glasses
'... the one with glasses'

Thus, both *di* and *cun* in ABS can be treated as functional prepositions. In this respect, they both head complementizer-like structures and are generated higher in the DP shell so that they become independent from the ellipsis process.

6.5. Conclusion

A comprehensive analysis of ABS and stSp N-drop phenomena has led us to a unified model that not only accounts for the data but also sheds light on internal DP structures; in particular, on the locus of phi-features interpretation and theta-role assignments.

Ellipsis operations are claimed to be universal and to apply uniformly across languages. What changes is the feature-specification of lexical and functional items (see also Borer 1984). In the cases under consideration, the features of determiners and prepositions seem to play a critical role in allowing or blocking N-drop.

7

Gender and Number Agreement

7.0. Introduction

This chapter provides a formal account for processes of gender and number agreement in the Afro-Bolivian Spanish DP. Cross-dialectal differences between Afro-Bolivian Spanish and standard Spanish are explained in light of the Minimalist Program/Principles and Parameter framework. In line with recent works on the structure of DP (Carstens 2000) and on how valuation processes are obtained (Pesetsky & Torrego 2007), I explain why certain agreement configurations are allowed in ABS, while they represent ungrammatical constructions in standard Spanish (stSp).

7.1. Data

With respect to what pertains to traditional ABS DP gender-agreement, grammaticality judgments and oral questionnaires indicated the presence of a configuration starkly different from the one encountered in stSp. In fact, the eldest speakers' intuitions indicated that gender agreement appears only on definite articles, while the rest of the DP elements show default-masculine concord (134).

(134)

    a. ABS: Todo la comida delicioso.
        all-M.SG the-F.SG food-F.SG delicious-M.SG
        stSp: Toda la comida deliciosa.
        all-F.SG the-F.SG food-F.SG delicious-F.SG
        'All the delicious food.'

    b. ABS: Este/eje comida delicioso.
        this/that-M.SG food-F.SG delicious-M.SG
        stSp: Esta/esa comida deliciosa.
        this/that-M.SG food-F.SG delicious-F.SG
        'This/that delicious food.'

As far as grammaticality judgments for number features are concerned, in traditional ABS, differently from stSp, plurality is marked only on determiners.

(135)

    a. ABS: Mis buen amigo boliviano.
        my-PL good-M.SG friend-M.SG Bolivian-M.PL
        stSp: Mis buenos amigos bolivianos.
        my-PL good-M.PL friend-M.PL Bolivian-M.PL
        'My good Bolivian friends.'

    b. ABS: Ejes buen amigo boliviano.
        this-M.PL good-M.SG friend-M.SG Bolivian-M.SG
        stSp: Esos buenos amigos bolivianos.
        this-M.PL good-M.PL friend-M.PL Bolivian-M.PL
        'These good Bolivian friends.'

As shown by examples (134–135), number and gender features are present in traditional ABS; nevertheless, number and gender marking is limited to certain DP elements. Therefore, in stark contrast with stSp, where all DP elements carry overt number and gender marking, in ABS these features are marked non-redundantly.

7.2. Agree and Agreement

In Chomsky's (2000) terms, overt morphological agreement is the result of the application of a formal operation: Agree. Agree applies in narrow syntax when an unvalued instance of a feature F (probe) c-commands another instance of F (goal). This probe-goal relation serves the purpose of deleting uninterpretable features (*uF[ ]*), which cannot be read at LF and must be eliminated before Spell-Out in order not to cause the derivation to crash. For this reason, Agree is seen as a case of feature assignment, which can be summarized in the following steps:

(136) Agree (Assignment version; following Chomsky 2000, 2001)

   (i)   An unvalued feature F (a *probe*) on a head H scans its
         c-command domain for another instance of F (a *goal*) with
         which to agree.
   (ii) If the goal has a value, its value is assigned as the value of
         the probe.

The operation Agree serves the purpose of deleting uninterpretable features, which are unreadable at the interfaces. Deletion takes place in a cyclical fashion at the end of each phase. Uninterpretable features, however, cannot be deleted during the syntactic derivation just by virtue of the fact that they cannot be interpreted at LF. The only means that the framework has to eliminate such features is to assume a biconditional relation correlating unvalued features with uninterpretable ones (137):

(137) Valuation/Interpretability Biconditional (Chomsky 2001: 5)
      A feature F is uninterpretable if F is unvalued.

By recurring to (137), the model can now delete uninterpretable features because they are unvalued and therefore act as probes. Such a stipulation inevitably leads us to the conclusion that once an uninterpretable feature has been valued, it will also get automatically deleted. Chomsky's Agree operation is therefore a syntactic mechanism of 'feature assignment,' triggered during the derivation by an unvalued-valued (probe-goal) relation, which, by virtue of a feature-biconditional requirement, results in the cyclical deletion of uninterpretable features before Spell-Out.

Chomsky's (2000, 2001) proposal has been revisited and refined by Pesetsky & Torrego (2007), among others—see, for example, Frampton & Gutmann (2000). In fact, recent work on Agree advocates a version of this operation that departs from the previous view of 'feature assignment' mechanism. Rather, the process is seen as an instance of 'feature sharing,' an idea in line with the view of agreement as feature unification common in HPSG

(Pollard & Sag 1994). Within the probe-goal theory of the syntactic computation, the operation Agree has been reformulated as in (138).

(138) Agree (Pesetsky & Torrego 2007)
    (i) An unvalued feature F (a *probe*) on a head H at syntactic location a (Fa) scans its c-command domain for another instance of F (a *goal*) at location b (Fb) with which to agree.
    (ii) Replace Fa with Fb, so that the same feature is present in both locations.

If a goal is valued for F, replacing the token-value of the probe with the value of the goal results in an instance of valued F substituting for the specification of the unvalued probe. A valued F may now serve as the goal for some ulterior operation of Agree triggered by an unvalued, higher instance of F serving as a new probe. The result is that a single feature F will be shared by several positions, and the process could iterate further.

Pesetsky and Torrego's proposal is different from Chomsky's approach not only in its feature-sharing view of Agree, but also in the absence of the Valuation/Interpretability Biconditional in (137). By removing this last constraint, the authors postulate the presence of features containing combinations of properties not available in the model previously suggested by Chomsky: (i) uninterpretable but valued; and (ii) interpretable but unvalued.

Lexical entries can now enter the derivation with four different kinds of features:

(139) Types of features (boldface = disallowed in Chomsky [2000, 2001])

    *u*F *val* **uninterpretable, valued**   *i*F *val* interpretable, valued
    *u*F [ ] uninterpretable, unvalued   *i*F [ ] **interpretable, unvalued**

This new framework, which stipulates the independence of valuation and interpretability, seems to be validated by several syntactic phenomena: the relationship between Tns and the finite verb, the formation of an interrogative CP, the formation of a declarative CP that supports successive-cyclic *wh*-movement; etc. Pesetsky & Torrego (2007) illustrate this approach by explaining how the relationship between Tns and the finite verbs is obtained.

In fact, an example of an interpretable unvalued feature acting as a probe is the T feature of the category Tns. In line with Pollock (1989), who posited a distinct Tns node as the locus of semantic tense interpretation, an uninterpretable feature that participates in an Agree relation with the T feature on Tns has been postulated for languages in which finite verbs bear morphological tense markers. Since Tns c-commands the finite verb, its T feature will act as a probe. For this reason, the T feature on Tns is seen as an interpretable unvalued feature searching for a goal, represented by the T feature on the finite verb, which is uninterpretable but valued:

(140) The relationship between Tns and the finite verb
    Agree
    . . . Tns . . . [*v* walked] . . . . . . Tns . . . [*v*walked]
    *i*T[ ]   *u*T +past   *i*T[2]   *u*T +past[2]

Nevertheless, the authors do not completely reject Chomsky's model. They maintain that Agree serves the purpose of deletion to avoid a crash in the derivation. At the same time, they share Brody's view on *Radical Interpretability*, which states the following:

(141) Thesis of Radical Interpretability (Brody 1997)
    Each feature must receive a semantic interpretation in some syntactic location.

Therefore, if all features must have an interpretation at a certain point, it follows that what is deleted is not the feature itself, but rather its uninterpretable instances. Radical Interpretability and the feature sharing framework provide an account for the fact that an uninterpretable valued feature (like [*u*T *val*] on the finite verb) must enter an Agree relation with an interpretable counterpart ([*i*T [ ]] on Tns). In fact, if this Agree relation could not be obtained, then the T feature could not receive an interpretation in any syntactic location, thus violating the thesis of Radical Interpretability.

7.3. Applying the Theory to the Data

Before entering into the details of this analysis, it is important to mention that I am assuming the DP structure provided in (142); where the loci of interpretation for person, number, and gender are D°, Num°, and N°, respectively (see also Carstens 2000).

(142)

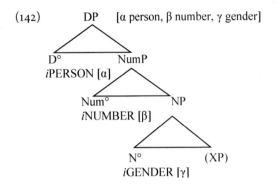

However, it must be kept in mind that because of the elimination of Valuation/Interpretability Biconditional (Pesetsky & Torrego 2007), I am not claiming that such interpretational loci will always come from the lexicon valued in ABS and stSp. In fact, the assumption is that in ABS, N enters the derivation with a value for gender [γ] and one for person [α], while Num carries a value for number [β] and D lacks person value [α]. On the other hand, in stSp N introduces into the derivation all phi-values [α], [β], and [γ], so that Num and D do not introduce valued features into the derivation.

In order to account for the presence of plural morphology on English nouns, Chomsky (2000, 2001) postulates the presence of a valued interpretable number feature on this element. By assuming such valued number specification, all DP entries specified for an unvalued uninterpretable number feature would be able to probe for it, in line with the c-command restriction imposed by Agree. On the other hand, if a higher element were bearing the interpretable feature, N would not be able to c-command such value and its overt morphological marking could not be explained.

However, Chomsky's postulation has been criticized because it fails to identify Num as the locus of number interpretability (Carstens 2000; Picallo 2008), contrary to what generally is assumed in the literature. Nevertheless, if we hold to the Valuation/Interpretability Biconditional and accept that number is interpretable in Num, Agree cannot account, at least in stSp, for some crucial morphological facts: First, there is no way to account for plural marking on N; second, postnominal adjectives, which are generally believed to be based generated in projections lower than NumP (Cinque 1994), should not carry number morphology either.

A way to circumvent such problems would consist of resorting to a different operation, Concord (Carstens 2000; Demonte 2008), which does not depend on c-command. On the other hand, Franceschina (2005) has suggested an ad hoc co-indexation between N and the postnominal A, so that when N moves to Num, the noun and the adjective will simultaneously agree and get identical number value.[1] Arguably, such moves are undesirable, since they eliminate any generalization of agreement.

As far as the valuation of number and gender features in the Spanish DP is concerned, the elimination of the Valuation/Interpretability Biconditional seems to account perfectly for the data. In fact, if we postulate that N contains an interpretable valued gender feature and an uninterpretable valued number feature, while Num contains an interpretable unvalued number specification, all DP elements become able to probe a gender and number value from N while obeying the principle of c-command.

Pesetsky and Torrego do not provide a detailed explanation of how such a reconfiguration would be implemented in the Spanish DP. They limit themselves to suggest that locating [inum] on Num and the number value on N would provide an explanation for Latin *pluralia tantum* nouns (Pesetsky & Torrego 2007: 264 n. 1). Therefore, to provide a better account of how the syntactic framework adopted here works in stSp, we may analyze the derivation of a stSp DP (143) (see Franceschina 2005 for a similar analysis).

(143) stSp: Esas pequeñas casas rojas
   this-F.PL small-F.PL house-F.PL red-F.PL
   'These small red houses.'

The noun *casa-* 'house' is specified for an uninterpretable valued number feature [unum: +PL], an interpretable valued gender feature [igen: +F], and an uninterpretable valued person feature [upers: + third]; it enters the derivation and merges with *n*. After the Merge operation has applied, N raises and adjoins to *n*.

(144)

n'
├── n
└── NP
     casa-
     [igen:+F]
     [unum:+PL]
     [upers:+3rd]

---

1. Franceschina (2005: 87 n.14) remains uncommitted about the exact implementation of this operation.

In line with Cinque (1994), I assume that post-nominal adjectives are merged at this point of the derivation; while pre-nominal ones are merged higher in the structure. Therefore, the first AP (*roj-*) is merged in the specifier projected by *n*. Subsequently, the uninterpretable unvalued number and gender specifications ([*u*num:], [*u*gen:]) carried by A act as probes and scan their local c-command. These features get valued resulting in the "sharing" of the number and gender values between N and A (see Frampton & Gutmann 2000).

(145)

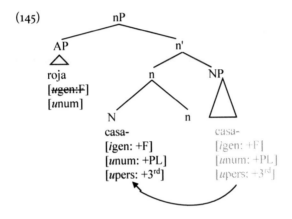

The nP so far created will merge with Num. In line with Carstens (2000) and Picallo (2008), Num is assumed to be the locus of number interpretation. Therefore, it bears an interpretable unvalued number feature ([*i*num:]), which acts as a probe and gets valued. N moves to Num, Num projects a specifier, which hosts the second AP (*pequeñ-*). From this position, its *u*num and *u*gen features act as probes and the Agree operation applies again.

(146)

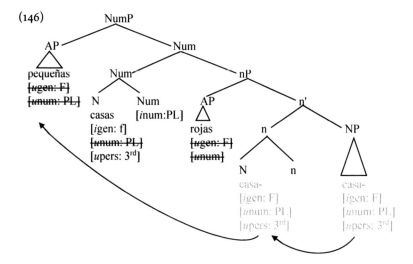

As a final point, example (147) illustrates how the D head is merged and its unvalued phi-features probe for a value. This process results in the valuation—and deletion—of all uninterpretable number features, which—if not eliminated—would cause the derivation to crash at the point of Spell-Out.

(147)

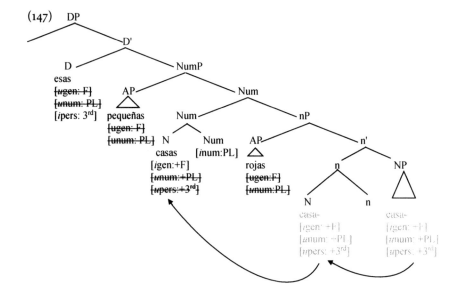

The system so far provided seems to work perfectly for stSp, where gender and number are marked redundantly across all the DP elements. Nevertheless, this model, given the c-command restriction on Agree and the valued number feature on N, cannot account for the ABS data. In fact, all stSp demonstratives, quantifiers, nouns, and articles come from the lexicon with a specification for number and gender features. Such specification, as shown in (144–147), is what will result in overt number and gender morphological marking after all the Agree operations have applied. On the other hand, traditional ABS does not possess the richness in feature specification characteristic of stSp and other Romance languages. In traditional ABS, nouns are specified for gender; this feature is not morphologically marked on the majority of the DP elements (it only appears on definite articles). Also, the morphological distribution of number marking is much more restricted; it is limited to determiners, and it never applies to adjectives, nouns, and quantifiers.

The ABS counterpart of (143) is (148).

(148) ABS: Ejes pequeño casa rojo.
this-M.PL small-M.SG house-F.SG red-M.SG
'These small red houses.'

As we want to keep syntactic processes constant and universal (Brody 2003),[2] neither ad hoc modifications to the operation Agree nor the introduction of special mechanisms to account for the data are available options. Nevertheless, the theory offers a different solution to this problem. Within the Minimalist Program framework, an account of cross-linguistic variation can be found in the different distribution of feature specifications among the lexical entries of the varieties under analysis. Therefore, to account for constructions like (148) in ABS, we may postulate that in this language, contrary to stSp, nouns only carry interpretable valued gender features and uninterpretable valued person ones, so that they are not specified for number. On the other hand, Num is the element carrying interpretable valued number features; D bears uninterpretable unvalued number features and interpretable unvalued person ones; while adjectives do not have any specifications for phi-features. In other words, traditional ABS DP elements lack many of the unvalued uninterpretable features encountered on their stSp counterparts. Such a deficiency results in the default singular and default masculine mor-

---

2. Brody refers to that as 'perfect syntax.'

phological realizations, so that the stSp example (147) can be derivationally represented as (149) for ABS.

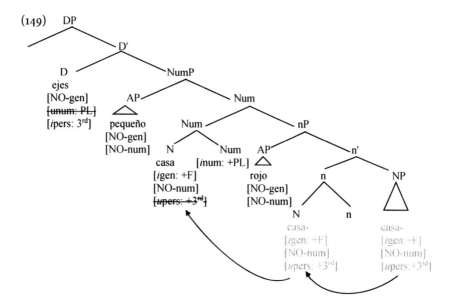

Besides the difference in feature specification between the two varieties, it is important to state another clear parametric distinction: in ABS the number value enters the derivation as a specification of Num (i.e., [*i*num: +/–PL]); in stSp it is carried by N. Note that this parametric distinction could arguably also be postulated for the contrast in number marking found between standard Brazilian Portuguese (stBP) (redundant plural marking) and popular Brazilian Portuguese (pBP) (non-redundant plural marking), where constructions like (150) are grammatical (see Simioni 2007).

(150) pBP: As casa vermelha.
the-F.PL house-F.SG red-F.SG
stBP: As casas vermelhas.
the-F.PL house-F.PL red-F.PL
'The red houses.'

Moreover, note that ABS poverty of feature specifications does not prevent this language from presenting the same adjective+noun and noun+adjective order combinations encountered in other Romance languages. In fact, as Carstens (2001: 154) and Alexiadou (2001: 223), among others, have demonstrated, raising of N to Num is not prompted by number feature checking, but rather by other mechanisms such as EPP or categorial features. This indicates that agreement, at least in these clear examples, cannot feed movement. In sum, the model proposed can account for important parametric differences between stSp and ABS—and potentially also between stBP and pBP. More cross-linguistic research is definitely needed to make a broader generalization. Nevertheless, the framework and the data seem highly promising.

7.4. Conclusion

This chapter has provided an overview of the distribution of phi-features across the ABS and the stSp DPs. Results indicate that while the computational operation Agree (Chomsky 2000) is constant and presumably universal, overt cross-dialectal variation is due to differences in the lexicon, namely in the feature specification of the elements entering the numeration. Based on the parametric differences encountered between stSp and ABS, I proposed an implementation of the Agreement framework able to account for the data.

Variation in the Determiner Phrase

8.0. Introduction

This chapter analyzes variable number and gender agreement marking across the Afro-Bolivian Spanish (ABS) Determiner Phrase (DP). As I indicated in chapter 2, African slavery persisted in Bolivia until 1826, when, with the implementation of the new constitution, slaves were declared free (Brockington 2006). Nevertheless, in practice, black Bolivians had to work as unpaid peons until 1952, year of the Land Reform. Only after that date did black Bolivians become free people and acquire the right to vote and to receive an education (Crespo 1995). Basic public education was introduced in Yungan communities in 1957; this factor, in addition to the higher degree of mobility achieved by black Bolivians after the end of the *hacienda* system, provoked a gradual decrease in use of the traditional dialect spoken by Afro-Bolivians. This process has been described as a systematic substitution of stigmatized basilectal ABS features with more prestigious stSp ones (Lipski 2006a, b). As far as ABS gender/number marking is concerned, this substitution is not random. Rather, what can be observed is the transition from one agreement system to another, according to specific syntactic constraints.

The focus of the present chapter is on the linguistic implications of this transition. In line with several sociolinguistic studies (Guy 1981; Poplack 1979, 1980; Scherre 2001; etc.), this chapter provides detailed VARBRUL statistical analyses for the cases of gender/number agreement marking variability found in this dialect. However, differently from traditional sociolinguistic accounts, results are explained by adopting recent minimalist assumptions on agreement and feature valuation processes (Frampton & Gutmann 2000). In doing so, the present chapter attempts to enhance dialogue between variationist sociolinguistics and generative theory.

8.1. Methodology

While the study of intra-speaker variation has long been one of the core topics of sociolinguistic research (Labov 1972), generative studies have traditionally paid less attention to this aspect of natural language. Intra-speaker variation, in fact, has often been considered an instance of E(xternal)-language, related to performance, thus not relevant to the core syntactic competence of the speaker and therefore, for the most part, ignorable (Chomsky 1986).

However, more recent generative proposals (Adger 2006; Adger & Smith 2005; Parrott 2007), developed within the architecture provided by the Minimalist Program (Chomsky 1995), postulate that variation may be accounted for as the overt result of covert lexical selections. This idea departs significantly from the notion of variable rules (e.g., Cedergren & Sankoff 1974), where probabilities could be built into the grammar itself (Labov 1972). Nevertheless, it represents a great step forward in attempting to reconcile the 'biological' and 'social' aspects of natural language (e.g., Cornips & Corrigan 2005).

In recent years, the combination of formal and sociolinguistic methodologies has led to a great number of fine-grained, empirically-testable generalizations (e.g., Cornips & Poletto 2005). In order to conduct research of this kind, it is crucial to gather both grammaticality judgments as well as naturalistic data. For this reason, the informants who participated in the present study were first interviewed and only later asked for grammaticality judgments. This was done in order to not influence the speakers during the interview by revealing in advance the nature of the linguistic phenomena under inspection.

When speakers of highly stigmatized languages are asked for grammaticality judgments, their answers may be partially influenced by the prescriptive notions they hold. Asking for grammaticality judgments in an indirect way may help overcome this problem (see Labov 1984). Thus, to discover whether or not a variable was present in the community, not only the direct intuitions were elicited—'Is X a grammatical construction?' 'Can you say X?'—also indirect questions were asked—'Is variant X present in this community?' 'Do you know anybody who can say X?' (Cornips & Poletto 2005: 944).

The comparison of these two different sources of data resulted in the interesting—but not unexpected—finding that almost everybody who claimed not to say X, but to know people who could say it, were found using X several times during the naturalistic interview. This would indicate that such a structure was indeed part of their grammar and confirmed the importance of relying on different sources. While grammaticality judgments can give us a good insight into the abstract idealized language of an informant, only a comparison of such information with empirical data can help us build a robust generalization.

My informants for this analysis consisted of twelve speakers of ABS. All of them were born and raised in the communities of Mururata, Chijchipa, and Tocaña, three small villages in the rural surroundings of Coroico, Department of La Paz, Bolivia. The speakers belonged to three different generations (21–50, 51–80, 80+). All the speakers reported for generation 80+ were illiterate, all those belonging to group 51–80 attended a few years of primary school, and all the speakers interviewed for the 21–50 age group had completed secondary education courses. As a consequence of this overlap between level of education and age, the language used by the youngest generation approximated more closely to standard Spanish than the one used by the older groups, particularly by the generation 80+, whose speakers showed the most significant divergences from standard Spanish.

8.2. Qualitative Data

An interesting discovery of my fieldwork was to find out that the informants participating in the study had diverging grammatical intuitions on DP gender agreement. All twelve Afro-Bolivian speakers interviewed indicated that in the most basilectal variety of this dialect gender agreement appears only on singular definite articles, while the remaining determines and adjectives show default-masculine morphology (151). Nevertheless, none of my speakers claimed to use this kind of language pattern. They considered it as an old dialect, which is not commonly heard these days.[1]

---

1. Lipski (2008: 82) suggests that ABS *lu* derives from stSp *los*. It results from the combination of two recurrent phonological rules in ABS: (1) the loss of final /s/; (2) the rising of unstressed /o/ to [u]. During his fieldwork, the author encountered some examples where *lu*

(151)

    a.   Todo la comida delicioso.
        all-M.SG the-F.SG meal-F.SG delicious-M.SG
        'All the delicious food.'

    b.   Todo lu comida delicioso.
        all-M.SG the-M.PL meal-F.SG delicious-M.SG
        'All the delicious foods.'

    c.   Este/eje comida delicioso.
        this/that-M.SG meal-F.SG delicious-M.SG
        'This/that delicious food.'

    d.   Mucho/un comida delicioso.
        much/a-M.SG meal-F.SG delicious-M.SG
        'Much/a delicious food.'

One subject in his 80s presented gender agreement also on plural definite articles and demonstratives (152), but not on other categories:

(152)

    a.   Todo la comida delicioso.
        all-M.SG the-F.SG meal-F.SG delicious-M.SG
        'All the delicious food.'

    b.   Todo las comida delicioso.
        all- M.SG the-F.PL meal-F.SG delicious-M.SG
        'All the delicious foods.'

    c.   Esta/esa comida delicioso.
        this/that-F.SG meal-F.SG delicious-M.SG
        'This/that delicious food.'

Informants with an age ranging from 51 to 84 (7/12) used agreement on plural and singular definite articles, demonstratives, pre-nominal adjectives, and also on weak quantifiers (153):

(153) Mucha/ una comida delicioso.
      much/a-F.SG meal-F.SG delicious-M.SG
      'Much/a delicious food.'

---

was used with singular nouns (e.g., *lu juamía* 'the family'). He, therefore, hypothesizes that in the early stages of formation ABS might have had *lu* as the only single definite article, for both singular and plural reference. This might well have been the case; nevertheless, I am not in the position of either confirming or rejecting this statement, since none of my informants was aware of the singular use of *lu*.

Finally, the youngest group, composed of four people from 21 to 50 years of age, used gender agreement for all the elements, including *todo* and postnominal adjectives (154):

(154) Toda la comida deliciosa.
　　　all-F.SG the-F.SG meal-F.SG delicious-F.SG
　　　'All that delicious food.'

This would intuitively lead us to argue in favor of four different grammars; however, a closer look at the empirical data from the oral interviews complicates the picture. In fact, it was common for somebody to claim to speak a certain grammar but use patterns belonging to another. Sometimes, speakers would freely alternate between forms within the same sentence. For example, the conversation fragment in (155) is from an informant whose grammaticality judgments indicated a grammar of type (154):

(155) Todo la comunidad participaba; mucha
　　　all-M.SG the-F.SG community-F.SG participated much-F.SG

　　　gente venía, mucho gente venía desde
　　　people-F.SG came much-M.SG people-F.SG came from

　　　lejos. Todas, toditas las personas se reunían.
　　　far all-F.PL all-F.PL the-F.PL people-F.SG reflex met

　　　Muy bonito la fiesta era . . .
　　　very nice-M.SG the-F.SG party-F.SG was

　　　"All the community used to participate, many people used to come, many people used to come from far away. All, all the people gathered. The party was very nice . . ."

Speakers like this present gender agreement on strong quantifiers in 50–60 percent of instances, thus indicating that cases of agreement mismatches are very common and should not be regarded as just E-language errors. On the other hand, as far as grammaticality judgments for number features are concerned, less variability was reported; nevertheless, much alternation could still be found when analyzing the transcripts from the naturalistic interviews. In fact, all informants, even the oldest ones, seem to be aware of the fact that, in traditional ABS, number is marked non-redundantly, as in (156), while 'at school' or more generally in stSp, it is marked on all the DP elements (157). No one, for example, claimed to inflect nouns while keeping post-nominal adjectives bare or vice versa.

(156) ABS
　　Mis/ejes/lu/mucho/cuatro buen plato tradicional.
　　My-PL/this-PL/the-PL/much-SG/four good.SG dish.SG
　　traditional.SG
　　'My/these/the/many/four good traditional dishes.'

(157) stSp
　　Mis/esos/los/muchos/cuatro buenos platos tradicionales.
　　My.PL/this.PL/the.PL/much.SG/four good.PL dish.PL
　　traditional.PL
　　'My/these/the/many/four good traditional dishes.'

Nevertheless, besides the clear grammatical intuitions distinguishing ABS from stSp plural marking, the corpus used for the study of number agreement—composed of the interviews with the three eldest members of the community—reveals several additional patterns, which are neither limited to the traditional marking of plurality on one single element in the DP, nor to the marking of all DP elements, as in stSp. In fact, also in regard to number agreement, speakers would use different forms variably (158). In cases like these, where the rate of mismatch is around 40 percent, it is arguably difficult to draw a clear line between what can be considered as competence and what can be labeled as performance.

(158) ABS
　　Lu pequeño se ha muerto, mis hijas
　　The-M.PL small-M.SG reflex AUX died-SG my-PL daughter-F.PL

　　jovena también se ha muerto. Mis hijo se ha muerto.
　　young-F.PL too reflex AUX died my-PL son-M.SG reflex AUX
　　died-SG

　　uno vivía aquí, uno a la Argentina.
　　one-M.SG lived here one-M.SG to the-F.SG Argentina-F.SG

　　'The kids died, my daughters died too. My sons died. One of them lived here, the other in Argentina.'

8.3. Quantitative Data

Previous attempts to formalize similar cases of variation have often recurred to stylistic features. One such case, which appears to be highly relevant to the present study, is exemplified by DeCamp's (1971: 352–53) generative analysis of the post-creole speech continuum. Faced with the amount of variability found in creole and post-creole contexts, the author admits the need to integrate the concept of systematic variation into the generative framework. While he indicates that certain phenomena have to do with performance (e.g., limitation on memory span, momentary lapses and reformulations, etc.), he indicates that there is room in the competence side of language for rule-governed variability:

> The ratio of passive to active sentences in my speech in a given day, the median length and complexity of my sentences, the frequency with which I deviate from grammatical well-formedness, these are performance features and cannot be reduced to the same type of rules found in generative grammars. But some kinds of variation are indeed rule-governed behavior. If I shift into a formal, oratorical style, several rule-predictable things happen to my grammar: the contraction transformation is blocked, so that I say *is not* and *he has* instead of *isn't* and *he's*, [. . .]. I am performing a complex but related set of switching activities, all triggered by the presence of one stylistic feature [+ oratorical].

Also, a similar formalization is postulated by Henry (2005), who recurs to [+/– formal] stylistic features to account for cases of subject-verb (dis) agreement in Belfast English. In formal situations, speakers would use a grammar for which the forms *there is/there are* require agreement, while for informal situations a different grammar would allow the verb to not agree with the subject, thus resulting in the default singular construction.

These accounts are not able to explain what is observed in ABS. In fact, within the one-hour interview period I had with my informants, the switches between the four potential parallel gender grammars were so many for certain individuals that no formal/informal style alternation might serve as a reasonable justification. Cross-generational VARBRUL results for internal factors (Table 8.1; see also Sessarego & Gutiérrez-Rexach 2011) indicate that the unvalued gender-feature distribution among grammatical categories is highly variable (Range 72): post-nominal adjectives disagree the most (Factor Weight .95), while plural and singular definite articles show the

Table 8.1
Variable Rule Analysis of Gender Agreement Variation in the Afro-Bolivian Spanish DP

Grammatical Category	Factor Weight	% Lack Agreement	N	% Data
Post-Nom. Adj.	.95	50	272	19
Strong.Q.	.66	35	275	11
Pre-Nom. Adj.	.64	14	220	19
Indef. Art.	.62	12	280	11
WeakQ	.60	10	102	4
Dem.	.24	3	84	3
Def. Art.	.23	2	1,371	53
Range	72			

Note. Log likelihood = −624.215, Significance = 0.001, N = 2,604.

highest level of concord (Factor Weight .23). Additionally, if the data for plural marking are introduced into the picture, the number of potentially-competing grammars increases exponentially, thus further constraining the feasibility of such a proposal (see Table 8.2; see also Delicado-Cantero & Sessarego 2011).

In recent years, Lipski (2006 a, b; 2011 a, b) has tried to formalize the gender and number agreement variation encountered in the ABS DP within the Optimality Theory (OT) framework (see Prince & Smolensky 1993/2004). He has also proposed a Gradual Learning Algorithm (see Boersma 1997; Boersma & Hayes 2001; Tesar & Smolensky 1998), endowed with variable stochastic constraint weightings, to explain the apparent left-to-right cross-generational evolution of the agreement domain across the ABS DP.

Indeed, faced with the high rates of gender and number agreement mismatches found in his sociolinguistic interviews, Lipski (2006b: 9) has classified ABS as a case of "DP impoverished agreement." Lipski suggests that gender and number features in DP percolate up from the noun to the determiner, and eventually to the post-nominal element (see Grimshaw 1997). He notices that in his linguistic corpus no case of post-nominal gender concord is found unless pre-nominal elements agree, as shown in (159):

Table 8.2
Variable Rule Analysis of Number Agreement Variation in the Afro-Bolivian Spanish DP

Grammatical Category	Factor Weight	% Lack Agreement	N	% Data
Adjectives	.65	19	47	9
Nouns	.56	70	313	59
Determiners	.38	81	172	32
Range	27			

Note. Log likelihood = −287.688, Significance = 0.007, *N* = 532). Given the relatively reduced number of tokens for the number agreement variation analysis, some of the grammatical categories were collapsed together: Adjectives (Post-Nom. Adj. and Pre-Nom. Adj.), Nouns, and Determiners (Strong.Q, WeakQ., Indef. Art., Dem, and Def. Art.). This was done to obtain a distribution of the tokens capable of providing statistically significant results.

(159)
    a. *Una curva ancha*
        a-F.SG. curve-F.SG. large-F.SG.
    b. *Una curva ancho*
        a-F.SG. curve-F.SG. large-M.SG.
    c. *Un curva ancho*
        a-M.SG. curve-F.SG. large-M.SG.
    d. **Un curva ancho*
        a-M.SG. curve-F.SG. large-F.SG.
        'A large curve.'

My data, when analyzed cross-generationally, are generally in line with those reported by Lipski. However, an important difference can be noticed in the speech of several informants. Many speakers present almost a complete lack of gender agreement in strong quantifiers, as shown in (160) and also in examples (151–152):

(160)
    a. *Todo las cosa bonito*
        all-M.SG. the-F.PL. thing-F.SG. nice-M.SG.
        'All the nice houses.'
    b. *Todo la chica de Tocaña*
        all-M.SG. the-F.SG. girl-F.SG. of Tocaña
        'All girls from Tocaña.'

    c. *Todo la comunidad*
       all-M.SG. the-F.SG. community-F.SG.
       'All the community.'

    Cases like these seem to violate the pre-nominal to post-nominal perco-lation order, unless we postulate that strong quantifiers are elements exter-nal to the DP, and then we argue—independently—in favor of a different mechanism for the checking of the gender feature in languages where they agree in gender and number with N, like Standard Spanish. Additionally, the feature-percolation account of gender agreement runs into problems when compared with data from other Romance varieties in which post-nominal adjectives may agree with N and disagree with D (see Pomino & Stark 2009 for Fassano Ladin).

    Alternatively, one might propose a system with one or more Agreement Projections inside the DP and with the relevant displacement operations applied to agreeing elements so that they enter into a specifier-head rela-tion (Koopman 1997; Sportiche 1990). This type of approach would be prob-lematic too in that the number of internal Agreement Projections required would not be limited, and would most likely be established on an ad hoc basis. It also runs against recent minimalist ideas supporting the elimination of Agreement Projections (Chomsky 2002). For these reasons, an account of number and gender agreement based on a minimalist model seems more adequate to describe the phenomena encountered in ABS. In fact, within the minimalist framework, agreement is conceived as the result of valuation processes, which do not necessarily require movement but just a configura-tional feature checking mechanism (Picallo 2008).

8.4. A Formal Analysis

Traditionally, linguistic intra-speaker variation has never been a core topic in formal syntactic studies. Nevertheless, more recently, within the frame-work provided by the Minimalist Program, several scholars have taken into consideration variation beyond the usual parametric inter-language domain (Adger 2006; Adger & Smith 2005; Parrott 2007; etc.) by paying closer atten-tion to previously disregarded phenomena—considered to be cases of per-formance errors (Chomsky 1957).

    Recent proposals within the Minimalist program (Chomsky 2001, 2002) advocate for the distinction between interpretable and non-interpretable features. The former can be read at LF; thus they carry a semantic meaning; while the latter lack such a semantic contribution and are present to trigger the necessary operations during the derivation. Said uninterpretable features have to be matched via Agree and are finally deleted before Spell-Out. In this model, number and gender agreement involves the transmission or sharing of features with nominal origin to lexical items (adjectives) or to functional elements (articles, demonstratives, quantifiers). Determiners and adjectives do not come from the lexicon with a value for number/gender; the number/gender feature of determiners and adjectives is lexically unvalued, and gets valued as a consequence of a syntactic process of agreement with the phi-feature of the noun (Chomsky 2001).

As illustrated in chapter 7, I am adopting the notion of agreement proposed by Pesetsky & Torrego (2007). These authors, in line with Frampton & Gutmann (2000), have proposed a model where agreement is conceived as 'feature sharing.' Their formulation of the operation Agree ensures that a feature value, once introduced into the derivation, will be probed by all unvalued items c-commanding it, thus resulting in the sharing of such a value across probes. Pesetsky & Torrego (2007) also argue against Chomsky's (2001) Valuation/Interpretability Biconditional and provide a new annotation, which includes four possible feature specifications: two probes (i.e., uF [ ], iF [ ]) and two goals (i.e., uF val, iF val) for a given feature F (see section 7.2). Relevant to my present analysis is also the annotation of a category underspecified for a certain feature F as no-$F[$ $]$. In such a case, the given category will not be able to act as either a probe or a goal for Agree operations. Example (161) illustrates the feature-sharing process described above.

(161) Example of feature sharing across categories bearing an F specification

$uF[val]$ . . . . $iF[val]$ . . . . $uF[val]$ . . . . . . $uF[val]$ ✕ . . . no-$F[$ $]$

Therefore, if we postulate that an uninterpretable instance of a feature such as gender and number may be present in certain DP elements but absent in others, and that variation is the result of differences in the feature specification of certain items in the initial numeration, it follows that contrasts in overt syntax will be the result of differences in the computation of varying specifications. I propose an account of the different gender and number agreement configurations across DP strings in ABS that can be summarized in the following fashion:

(162) *Gender features valuation*

  a. [DP mucho   [NumP   [nP [NP comida   delicioso]]]]
      no-Gen[ ]................✕..............*iGen[F]*....✕....*no-Gen[ ]*

  b. [DP mucha   [NumP   [nP [NP comida   delicioso]]]]
      uGen[F]....................................*iGen[F]*....✕....*no-Gen[ ]*

  c. [DP mucha   [NumP   [nP [NP comida   deliciosa]]]]
      uGen[F]....................................*iGen[F]*..............*uGen[F]*

    'Much delicious food.'

(163) *Number features valuation*

  a. [DP mucho   [NumP [nP [NP plato   [AP tradicional]]]]]
      no-Num[ ].....✕......*iNum[PL]*...✕.......*no-Num[ ]*...✕..*no-Num[ ]*

  b. [DP muchos   [NumP [nP [NP plato   [AP tradicional]]]]]
      uNum[PL]..............*iNum[PL]*......✕......*no-Num[ ]*...✕..*no-Num[ ]*

  c. [DP muchos   [NumP [nP [NP platos   [AP tradicional]]]]]
      uNum[PL]..............*iNum[PL]*..............*uNum[PL]*..✕..*no-Num[ ]*

  d. [DP muchos   [NumP [nP [NP platos   [AP tradicionales]]]]
      uNum[PL]..............*iNum[PL]*..............*uNum[PL]*.........*uNum[PL]*

    'Many traditional dishes.'

This minimalist approach can account for all the agreement configurations found in the ABS Determiner Phrase by postulating the presence/absence of unvalued gender/number features on the different DP components. Results from cross-generational statistical analyses (Sessarego & Gutierrez-Rexach 2011) suggest that ABS is undergoing a cross-generational change in which stigmatized basilectal ABS features are being substituted by more prestigious stSp ones. One result of this transition is the introduction of a wider range of agreement configurations in a language that originally made little use of it. In minimalistic terms, this phenomenon can be seen as the emergence and development of unvalued features on elements that previously were not specified for them.

This analysis is capable of accounting for the agreement variability found in ABS, without postulating the existence of several competing grammars (e.g., DeCamp 1971; Henry 2005) or the presence of variable syntactic rules (Labov 1972). On the other hand, variation is limited to the presence/absence of uninterpretable features in lexical items. Note that, as pointed out by Adger & Smith (2005: 164), "this is a very minimal theory, since the idea that speakers have to choose lexical items is one which we simply cannot do without." At the same time, localizing morphosyntactic variation in the choice of lexical items implies that we do not need to postulate special mechanisms to deal with variation; rather "variation is precisely what we should expect" (Adger & Smith 2005: 164).

The presence of identical lexical entries differing only in their uninterpretable feature specification may be considered as a case of morphological doublets *à la* Kroch (1994). In fact, in Kroch's view, the historical evolution of competing morphological doublets (different elements with the same morphological function occurring in the same context) is diachronically unstable: either the two forms specialize, and therefore stop being doublets, or "one form tends to drive the other out of use and so out of the language" (Kroch 1994: 17). This would be due to the "Blocking Effect" (Aronoff 1976), which does not allow morphological doublets. The blocking effect, in Kroch's words, does not prevent doublets from arising in a language through social processes (e.g., language contact). Rather, it acts as an economy constraint on their storage. Therefore, morphological doublets are frequently found in natural language but they are diachronically unstable. 'Blocking,' in Kroch's words, is the process by which the "languages always evolve [. . .] in such a way that one or the other variant becomes extinct" (1994: 4). This seems to capture what is happening in ABS, where alternating forms can be frequently encountered in the speech of the same informant, and where this Afro-Hispanic vernacular appears to be gradually transitioning from one agreement system to another.

8.5. The Local Agreement Gradience Function

Recall that findings from grammaticality judgments led to the identification of four different patterns of gender agreement (see 151–54). Nevertheless, there is a considerable amount of variability, thus indicating that agreement patterns are not completely stable. For this reason, certain ideas proposed by

Adger & Smith (2005) to account for unvalued uninterpretable features seem more adequate to capture the nature of the phenomena found in ABS. The nature of the element occurring with the nominal head (e.g. articles, adjectives, strong/weak quantifiers, etc.) has a clear effect on the output; however, not only computational factors condition the agreement operation, but also lexical ones seem to play a crucial role.

While grammaticality judgments were discordant for certain syntactic categories among informants, every participant agreed on the use of *el* and *la* as respectively the masculine singular definite article and the feminine singular definite one. Nevertheless, there are several cases indicating that certain nouns in ABS possess a different gender from the one found in their standard Spanish counterparts. For this reason, ABS *el* may appear with nouns that in standard Spanish are feminine, while ABS *la* may precede nouns that in standard Spanish are masculine.[2]

(164)

    a.   ABS: Ele dice que es el máximo autoridad.

          stSp: Él dice que es la máxima autoridad.

          'He says he is the maximum authority.'

    b.   ABS: La sistema de hacienda no sirve pa' nada.

          stSp: El sistema de hacienda no sirve para nada.

          'The hacienda system is useless.'

Gender mismatches on adjectives and determiners, when comparing ABS and stSp are common, with the masculine gender prevailing over the feminine one. I claim that these differences are due to two separate factors: (a) certain words listed in the stSp lexicon as feminine, are listed in the ABS as masculine and vice versa; (b) the valuation process in ABS departs from standard Spanish in that certain ABS elements lack the unvalued features present in their Spanish counterparts.

Several external factors may affect the item selection: age, education, social class, etc. (Adger & Smith 2005: 164). When looking at Table 8.3, we can observe that generation is, in fact, a significant factor group, with the oldest group (80+) strongly favoring lack of agreement (Factor Weight .67) and the 21–50 group disfavoring it (Factor Weight .35). These data reflect

---

2. The examples in (164) are instances of natural speech extracted from the sociolinguistic interviews of two elderly women (generation +80). When these speakers were asked for grammaticality judgments on such constructions, they indicated that the gender value of *sistema* 'system' was feminine and that of *autoridad* 'authority' was masculine.

Table 8.3

Cross-Generational Variable Rule Analysis of Gender Agreement Variation in the Afro-Bolivian Spanish DP

Generation	Factor Weight	% Lack Agreement	N	% Data
81+	.67	20	650	25
51–80	.56	17	937	36
21–50	.35	5	1,027	39
Range	32			

Note. Log likelihood = −624.215; Significance = 0.001; N = 2,604.

the presence of a cross-generational change, pushing ABS in the direction of stSp. Younger generations did not experience the segregation imposed by the *hacienda* system and had more opportunities to have contact with the Spanish spoken outside the community. These elements, in addition to the stigmatization attached to the Afro-Hispanic vernacular, are pushing the younger members of the community to quickly replace the basilectal features with more prestigious stSp ones.

Even though there are no wider diachronic data available, by looking at the synchronic results for the three generations under analysis, we can get an idea of how the gender-agreement domain might have expanded in ABS. The three relevant generations show three different levels of gender agreement. While for the +80 generation agreement is mainly limited to demonstratives, definite articles, weak quantifiers and pre-nominal adjectives; for the 51–80 generation, strong quantifiers also agree in the majority of instances. On the other hand, post-nominal adjectives agree in more than 50 percent of cases only for the 21–50-generation informants.

Gender agreement evolution seems to develop cross-generationally in a systematic way. In fact, for all three figures, the following gender agreement ranking holds across the grammatical categories analyzed (where < indicates earlier development and increased frequency):

(165) DEM/D < WEAK Q < PRE-N A < STRONG Q < POST-N A

This property, in addition to the fact that all singular definite articles agree with the noun in gender, might indicate that in a previous stage gender agreement was limited to singular definite articles, and it gradually extended

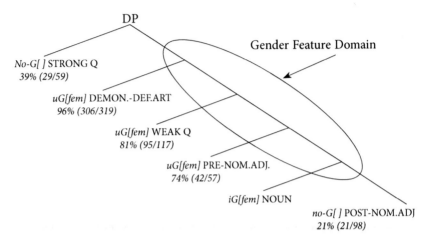

DP

No-G[ ] STRONG Q
39% (29/59)

uG[fem] DEMON.-DEF.ART
96% (306/319)

uG[fem] WEAK Q
81% (95/117)

uG[fem] PRE-NOM.ADJ.
74% (42/57)

iG[fem] NOUN

no-G[ ] POST-NOM.ADJ
21% (21/98)

Gender Feature Domain

Figure 8.1. Gender Agreement Patterns for 80+ Generation according to Grammatical Category (Percentages and Raw Numbers).

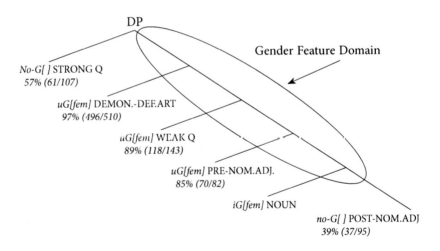

DP

No-G[ ] STRONG Q
57% (61/107)

uG[fem] DEMON.-DEF.ART
97% (496/510)

uG[fem] WEAK Q
89% (118/143)

uG[fem] PRE-NOM.ADJ.
85% (70/82)

iG[fem] NOUN

no-G[ ] POST-NOM.ADJ
39% (37/95)

Gender Feature Domain

Figure 8.2. Gender Agreement Patterns for 51–80 Generation according to Grammatical Category (Percentages and Raw Numbers).

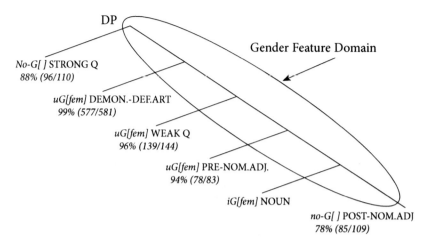

Figure 8.3. Gender Agreement Patterns for 21–50 Generation according to Grammatical Category (Percentages and Raw Numbers).

to the rest of the categories. Setting aside those mismatches that are due to different specifications in the lexicon, all the rest have to be viewed as the by-product of a specific locality constraint on gender agreement/valuation. This constraint is conditioned by the derivational position of the affected probes with respect to the nominal head. Additionally, I assume that pre-nominal adjectives agree because they are in the domain of the Q probes, either by direct insertion or movement (Gutiérrez-Rexach & Mallén 2001).

Interestingly, these findings are also in line with Second Language Acquisition (SLA) research on the acquisition of gender agreement in DP. In fact, Hawkins (1998) showed that English students speaking French as a second language presented more agreement on definite articles than on indefinite ones, and more agreement on determiners than on adjectives; similar findings have also been reported for English speakers of Spanish by Bruhn de Garavito & White (2000), and more recently by Franceschina (2005), who tested advanced speakers of Spanish coming from a variety of backgrounds (Italian, Portuguese, English, Arabic, German, and French). All these studies on gender agreement also share the common view that masculine is the default value, as it appears significantly more on determiners, and on adjectives in cases of agreement mismatches. These data indicate that language evolution follows certain hierarchical steps (see Pienemann 1998).

When we try to frame this analysis within current formal SLA models, we may recur to the framework proposed by Herschensohn (2000), Minimalist Constructionism. Minimalist Constructionism is an SLA model assuming that cross-linguistic variation is limited to the lexicon and to its formal features (Borer 1984), while syntax is universal and therefore invariable (Chomsky 1995). Within this framework, the locus of cross-linguistic variation is limited to the features of lexical and functional items. This model argues that the acquisition of L2 features is gained through a phase of L1–L2 transition. Constructionism is based on empirical evidence supporting the idea that languages are acquired *gradually*. This fact may be formalized by saying that, during the acquisition process, certain features, after having lost their L1 values, are unspecified and will incrementally gain new L2 values, thus giving rise to variation. This process consists of the progressive mastery of the target language functional and lexical categories, through the gradual acquisition of its lexicon (Herschensohn 2000: 81). Contrary to previous claims in SLA literature (e.g., Clahsen & Muysken 1986), within the constructionist framework, Universal Grammar (UG) is not only available during L1 acquisition; rather, it drives L2 development through a set of possible, acquirable grammars, thus suggesting that UG is fully accessible during L2 acquisition (see Epstein, Flynn, & Martohardjono 1996; Schwartz 1996, 1998; Schwartz & Sprouse 1996). In Herschensohn's words, "L2 grammars are constrained by universal principles in that intermediate and final state grammars are possible human languages" (2000: 80).

The advantage of this approach on previous generative attempts—such as the Principles & Parameters model—is that parameter resetting is no longer considered as the fundamental difference accounting for L1 vs. L2 development. Rather this distinction is now explained as an incomplete command over a language-particular lexicon that interfaces with the syntax. Instead of a 'yes/no' parameter switch, the gradual acquisition of the lexical and morphological features naturally accounts for the variability encountered in all second languages. L2 acquisition happens gradually and the most peripheral morpholexical items will be the last ones to be mastered since the learner constructs the "grammar from the core to the periphery" (Herschensohn 2000: 81).

Thus, by looking at our data on the progression of gender agreement in the ABS DP, we can formulate the following Local Agreement Gradience Function (LAGF), which provides us with an evolutionary "core-periphery" path for the development of uninterpretable gender features across the DP:

(i) If A and B are potential probes for feature F in goal G and B is closer (more local) to G than A, then AGREE can apply between A and G only if it applies between B and G. The closer a functional head is to the noun, the more likely it is to enter into an agreement (sharing) relation with it. Additionally, (ii) A functional element becomes a potential probe for F when it is specified as unvalued for F, and (iii) There is speaker variation with respect to the specification of F.

The main consequence of LAGF is that it predicts gradience of agreement in ABS: Definite Articles and Demonstratives are more likely to agree with N; Weak Quantifiers and Prenominal Adjectives are less likely; Strong Qs and Postnominal Adjectives are the least likely.

From a biolinguistic perspective, the data show how evolutionary dynamics meets dialectal variation: LAGF determines a coherence measure for performance differences in the candidate grammars of a population, consistent with Nowak's (2002) and Nowak, Komarova, & Niyogi's (2001) findings. Population and social dynamics move the convergence point (ideal fitness) of LAGF in ABS closer to standard Spanish. This eventually entails a generalized application of Agree/gender valuation within the DP in younger generations. The main consequence of this situation is that contact with HBS/standard varieties leads younger speakers to apply Agree to higher probes. Agreement is triggered when the relevant probe becames [uGen] rather than [No-Gen] (see Sessarego & Gutiérrez-Rexach 2012).

8.6. Conclusion

This chapter has offered a quantitative approach to variable agreement within the DP in Afro-Bolivian Spanish. My findings and proposal try to bridge the gap between the study of variationist and generativist studies. Variation is a component of human languages, and my results confirm that it should be taken into account when analyzing structural properties in specific syntactic domains, such as agreement in the DP. The goal here is to characterize the ingredients of variation in a structurally systematic fashion, as computationally determined by differences in the specification of lexical items and by restrictions on syntactic operations, more specifically, as a locality condition on agreement. Accounts of this sort are now possible after recent developments in the minimalist (and related) frameworks, which are trying to account for alternation and variation phenomena affecting syntactic elements (Adger & Smith 2005).

This research also unveils fundamental sociolinguistic issues. The underlying reasons pushing Afro-Bolivian in the direction of a more prestigious Spanish variety are essentially the stigmatization of the Afro-Hispanic vernacular and the increasing contact with a more prestigious Spanish dialect. Contact with Bolivian Spanish increased substantially after 1952, the year of the Bolivian Land Reform, which freed Afro-Bolivians from forced peonage and introduced education in the black communities. These changes, which have affected the socioeconomic scenario of black Bolivia during the last six decades, are reflected in the speech of the community members. This scenario would explain why 'generation' was proven to be a significant factor group affecting the studied variation. From a theoretical perspective, this study sheds some light on the linguistic constraints regulating agreement in an Afro-Hispanic vernacular approximating to a more prestigious Spanish dialect. The process is driven by social factors through a path that is highly constrained by syntactic ones.

Conclusion

Microparametric syntax is a growing field of research, which can be used as a tool to test formal syntactic theories (Barbiers & Cornips 2001). The field of syntactic microvariation has developed significantly during the last decade; particular attention has been paid to the study of microparametric variation across Italian, Dutch, and English dialects (see, for example, Adger & Smith 2005; Barbiers & Cornips 2001; Benincà 1989; Poletto 2000). So far, not many microparametric studies of this kind have been conducted on Spanish; in particular, Afro-Hispanic contact varieties have never been studied by adopting this approach. This opens up a new field of investigation, which, if addressed in a methodological and systematic way, could lead to interesting discoveries. The main purpose of this book was to create a foundation to build such a research program.

From a theoretical point of view, Afro-Hispanic contact varieties represent an important group of Spanish dialects. In fact, these languages are rich in constructions that would be considered ungrammatical in standard Spanish (stSp). For the most part, the varieties that developed in Latin America from the contact of African languages and Spanish at the time of slavery are not "radical creoles." Conversely, they present parametric configurations relatively similar to Spanish, but at the same time, they bear differences that can be traced back to fossilized second language acquisition strategies. Such dialectal differences provide researchers with a great linguistic laboratory

(Kayne 2000), where generative hypotheses, traditionally developed on the intuitions of standard language speakers, can be tested and evaluated against a different, but closely related, set of linguistic data.

In this work, my attention was primarily directed at two different objectives. The first goal was to shed light on the unclear origin of ABS by analyzing the available sociohistorical data as well as the linguistic evidence found in this language. The second goal was to explore certain aspects of the Afro-Bolivian Spanish (ABS) Determiner Phrase (DP) to provide a testing ground for verifying the feasibility of current linguistic hypotheses and, when appropriate, to propose new solutions in light of the empirical data collected.

As far as the origin of ABS is concerned, my findings indicate that ABS is a language that approximated Spanish from its inception and probably did not develop from the nativization of an earlier pidgin, as suggested by Lipski (2008). In fact, several factors have affected the dimension of African slavery in Bolivia and consequently the presence of a black population in the territory since the sixteenth century. We observed that the Spanish Crown's monopoly of slave trading, the geographic location of Bolivia, and the availability of a native workforce affected the cost of Africans, raising their price and, as a result, reducing the number and the dimension of slave transactions. The non-massive introduction of a black workforce into the territory favored the acquisition of a closer approximation to Spanish by the slaves. Moreover, the Yungan *hacienda* was not a plantation society of the kind found elsewhere in the Americas; it was characterized by low black/white ratio and relatively high social mobility. Linguistic findings suggest that the grammatical elements of ABS, which had been invoked in the literature as potential creole indicators, can also be ascribed to a conventionalized advanced second language, which probably crystallized in these rural valleys and did not undergo processes of standardization imposed elsewhere by urban society and the linguistic norm.

With respect to the second objective, the close proximity of ABS to stSp provided us with a great "syntactic testing lab." In particular, I focused on bare nouns, N-ellipsis, gender and number agreement processes and their variability. The study of ABS bare nouns revealed that Chierchia's (1998) Nominal Mapping Parameter does not hold. In fact, contrary to what is predicted by Chierchia, in this Afro-Hispanic vernacular bare singular nouns can appear in both subject and object positions, while definite articles, plural morphology, and lexicalized count/mass distinctions are present. We concluded that the so-called bare nouns in ABS are not actually bare; rather, they are embedded into a DP structure headed by an empty D head (in line

with Longobardi 1994). We saw that these nouns can take on several interpretations, depending on the syntactic, semantic, and pragmatic context in
which they appear.

As far as N-ellipses are concerned, some important parametric differences and similarities could be encountered between stSp and ABS. In fact,
comparison of the ABS and the stSp data indicated that even if ABS is not
inflectionally rich, it allows all the elliptical configurations encountered in
stSp. The examples provided also indicated that, in ABS, as well as in stSp,
gender, differently from number, is a feature of the noun, which gets deleted
in the process of elision. This fact appears to contradict approaches that postulate a unique projection for number and gender (e.g., Ritter 1991, 1993),
as well as those that argue in favor of two separate projections, NumP and
a GenP (e.g., Bernstein 1993, Picallo 1991). In fact, masculine and feminine
nouns do not seem to be derivable from the same lexical entry. Data, on the
other hand, back a framework in which lexical entries are clearly different
in gender specifications before entering the syntactic numeration. Therefore, only NumP is a licit projection while 'gender' is lexically specified in
N. Moreover, in this Afro-Hispanic dialect, nouns can often be elided also
in contexts for which an ungrammatical construction would obtain in stSp,
namely when the elided noun is followed by *cun* 'with.' A curious peculiarity, which might explain why *cun*-PP can licitly survive nominal ellipsis in
this vernacular, is that ABS *cun* is often used where *de* would be preferred in
stSp. As all elliptical patterns are the same in ABS and stSp with the exception of *cun/con* constructions, I assumed that this distinction must have to
do with such prepositions. This statement is justified, as *con/cun* presents
different grammatical behaviors in the two languages.

In contrast with some previous analyses (Ticio 2003, 2005), the model I
proposed attempted to avoid ad hoc post-syntactic movements and insertion operations. It agrees with other proposals (Kayne 1994; Kester & Sleeman 2002) in ascribing a special status to stSp *de* and *que*, namely the status
of complementizer heads, and based on the cross-linguistic data, it extends
such a generalization to ABS *di*, *que*, and *cun*.

Traditional ABS does not possess the richness in feature specification
characteristic of stSp and other Romance languages. In traditional ABS,
nouns are specified for gender, but this feature is not morphologically
marked on the majority of the DP elements (it only appears on singular
definite articles). Also, the morphological distribution of number marking
is much more restricted: it is limited to determiners, and it never applies to
adjectives, nouns, and quantifiers. For this reason, I suggested that in traditional ABS nouns do not carry number features at all, while Num enters

the derivation with a valued and interpretable number specification. These parametric differences between ABS and stSp shed some light on current debates concerning the role of Agree. Namely, we saw that ABS poverty of feature specifications does not prevent this language from presenting the same adjective+noun and noun+adjective order combinations encountered in Romance languages, thus suggesting that N raising is probably not triggered by phi-agreement.

The data collected through means of grammaticality judgments and sociolinguistic interviews indicated several different gender/number agreement patterns. The analysis of these variable data led us to depart from sociolinguistic models that propose the presence of variable rules (Labov 1972), as well as the frameworks that analyze variation in terms of competing grammatical systems (Kroch 1989), or as the alternation of formal/informal styles (DeCamp 1971; Henry 2005). Conversely, we embraced Adger & Smith's (2005) approach, which postulates that overt variability depends on covert lexical selection, where syntactic operations (Merge, Move, Agree) remain constant and universal (see Borer 1984; Chomsky 1995) Also, the study of cross-generational gender agreement evolution allowed the formulation of the Local Agreement Gradience Function (LAGF), which predicts a gradual development of uninterpretable feature specifications on the DP categories depending on their degree of proximity to N.

This book explored some aspects of the syntax of the ABS DP; it combined sociolinguistic techniques of data collection and generative models of analysis to obtain more fine-grained, empirically-testable generalization. This composite approach has proven very suitable to the formal study of a highly stigmatized dialect like Afro-Bolivian Spanish. While for the analysis of 'bare' nouns and N-ellipses I adopted a more traditional, formal methodology of data collection, which relied mainly on direct grammaticality judgments, for the study of gender and number agreement phenomena, I combined naturalistic data collection to the employment of indirect elicitations. This allowed us to strengthen the empirical bases of syntactic analysis and limit the influence of prescriptive pressure on the results (see Cornips & Poletto 2005; Labov 1984), thus unveiling the presence of syntactic constructions that would have otherwise remained hidden.

The present study represents the first microparametric work on an Afro-Hispanic contact variety. Afro-Hispanic dialects offer a great opportunity for microparametric studies; there is plenty to do for those who are willing to take on this challenge.

References

Abney, S. 1987. The noun phrase in its sentential aspect. PhD diss., MIT.

Adger, D. 2006. Combinatorial variability. *Journal of Linguistics* 42: 503–530.

Adger, D., & J. Smith. 2005. Variation and the minimalist program. In *Syntax and Variation: Reconciling the Biological and the Social,* eds. L. Cornips & K. P. Corrigan, 149–178. Amsterdam: Benjamins.

Adger, D., & G. Trousdale. 2007. Variation in English syntax: Theoretical implications. *English Language and Linguistics* 11(2): 261–278.

Alarcos-Llorach, E. 1973. *Estudios de gramática funcional del español.* BRH, Estudios y Ensayos, 147. Madrid: Gredos.

Alexiadou, A. 2001. Adjective syntax and noun raising: Word order asymmetries in the DP as the result of adjective distribution. *Studia Linguistica* 55(3): 217–248.

Álvarez, A., & E. Obediente. 1998. El español caribeño: Antecedentes sociohistóricos y lingüísticos. In *América negra: Panorámica actual de los estudios lingüísticos sobre variedades hispanas, portuguesas y criollas,* eds. M. Perl & A. Schwegler, 40–61. Madrid: Iberoamericana.

Andrés-Gallego, J. 2005. *La esclavitud en la America española.* Madrid: Ediciones encuentro.

Angola-Maconde, J. n. d. Unpublished manuscript. La Paz, Bolivia.

Arends, J. 2008. A demographic perspective on creole formation. In *The Handbook of Pidgin and Creole Studies,* eds. S. Kouwenberg & J. Singler, 309–331. Hoboken, NJ: Wiley-Blackwell.

Aronoff, M. 1976. *Word Formation in Generative Grammar.* Linguistic Inquiry Monograph, no. 1. Cambridge, MA: MIT Press.

Asher, N., & A. Lascarides. 1998. *Bridging: Journal of Semantics* 15(1): 83–113.

Auger, J. 1998. Le redoublement des sujets en français informel quebecois: Une approche variationiste. *Canadian Journal of Linguistics* 43(1): 37–63.

Bakker, P., A. Daval-Markussen, M. Parkvall, & I. Plag. 2011. Creoles are typologically distinct from non-creoles. *Journal of Pidgin and Creole Languages* 26(1): 5–42.

Baptista, M. 2007. On the syntax and semantics of DP in Cape Verdean Creole. In *Noun Phrases in Creole Languages*, eds. M. Baptista & J. Guéron, 61–106. Amsterdam: John Benjamins.

Barbiers, S. 2005. Word order variation in three verb clusters and the division of labor between generative linguistics and sociolinguistics. In *Syntax and Variation: Reconciling the Biological and the Social*, eds. L. Cornips & K. P. Corrigan, 233–264. Amsterdam: John Benjamins.

———. 2009. Locus and limits of syntactic microvariation. *Lingua* 119(11): 1607–1623.

Barbiers, S., & L. Cornips. 2001. Introduction to syntactic microvariation. In *Syntactic Microvariation*, eds. S. Barbiers, L. Cornips, & S. van der Kleij. 1–11. www.meertens.knaw.nl/projecten/sand/synmic/

Belletti, A., & L. Rizzi. 1988. Psych-verbs and Q-theory. *Natural Language and Linguistic Theory* 6: 291–352.

Bello, A. 1847. *Gramatica de la lengua castellana destinad a al uso de los americanos*. Santiago: Imprenta de Progreso.

Benincà, P. 1989. *Dialect Variation and the Theory of Grammar*. Dordrecht: Foris.

———. 1994. *La variazione sintattica: Studi di dialettologia romanza*. Bologna: Il Mulino.

Bernstein, J. 1993. The syntactic role of word markers in null nominal constructions. *Probus* 5: 5–38.

Bickerton, D. 1981. *Roots of Language*. Ann Arbor, MI: Karoma.

Bickerton, D., & A. Escalante. 1970. Palenquero: A Spanish-based creole of Northern Colombia. *Lingua* 13: 63–92.

Blackburn, R. 1997. *The Making of New World Slavery*. London: Verso.

Borer, H. 1984. *Parametric Syntax: Case Studies in Semitic and Romance Languages*. Dordrecht: Foris.

Boersma, P. 1997. How we learn variation, optimality, and probability. *Proceedings of the Institute of Phonetic Sciences of the University of Amsterdam* 21: 43–58.

Boersma, P., & B. Hayes. 2001. Empirical tests of the Gradual Learning Algorithm. *Linguistic Inquiry* 32: 45–86.

Bosque, I., & M. C. Picallo. 1996. Postnominal adjectives in Spanish DPs. *Journal of Linguistics* 32: 349–385.

Bouisson, E. 1997. Esclavos de la tierra: Los campesinos negros del Chota-Mira, siglos XVII–XX. *Procesos: Revista Ecuatoriana de Historia* 11: 45–67.

Bowser, F. 1974. *The African Slave in Colonial Peru, 1524–1650*. Stanford, CA: Stanford University Press.

Bridikhina, E. 1995a. El tráfico de esclavos negros a La Paz a fines del siglo xviii. *Estudios Bolivianos* 1: 183–191.

———. 1995b. *La mujer negra en Bolivia*. La Paz: Ministerio de Desarrollo Humano.

Brockington, L. 2006. *Blacks, Indians, and Spaniards in the Eastern Andes*. Lincoln: University of Nebraska Press.

Brody, M. 1997. Perfect chains. In *Elements of Grammar*, ed. L. Haegeman, 139–167. Dordrecht: Kluwer Academic Publishers.

———. 2003. *Lexico-logical form*. Cambridge, MA: MIT Press.

Brucart, J. M. 1987. La elisión sintáctica en español. PhD diss., Universitat Autònoma de Barcelona.

———. 1999. La elipsis. In *Gramática descriptiva de la lengua española*, eds. I. Bosque & V. Demonte, 2: 2787–2866. Madrid: Espasa.

Brucart, J. M., & M. L. Gràcia. 1986. I sintagmi nominali senza testa. *Rivista di Grammatica Generativa* 11: 3–32.

Bruhn de Garavito, J., & L. White. 2000. L2 acquisition of Spanish DPs: The status of grammatical features. In *Proceedings of the 24th Annual Boston University Conference on Language Development,* eds. C. Howell, S. Fish, & T. Keith-Lucas, 164–75. Somerville, MA: Cascadilla Press.

Busdiecker, S. 2006. We are Bolivians too: The experience and meaning of blackness in Bolivia. PhD diss., University of Michigan.

Cardinaletti, A., & G. Giusti. 1991. Partitive *ne* and the QP-Hypothesis: A case study. *University of Venice Working Papers in Linguistics* 1: 1–19.

Carlson, G. 1977. *Reference to kinds in English*. PhD diss., University of Massachusetts, Amherst.

Carstens, V. 2000. Concord in minimalist theory. *Linguistic Inquiry* 31(2): 319–355.

———. 2001. Multiple agreement and case-deletion: Against Φ-InCompleteness. *Syntax* 4: 147–163.

Cedergren, H. J., & D. Sankoff. 1974. Variable rules: Performance as a statistical reflection of competence. *Language* 50(2): 333–355.

Chambers, J. K. 2003. *Sociolinguistic Theory: Linguistic Variation and Its Social Implications.* Oxford: Blackwell.

———. 2004. Dinamic typology and vernacular universals. In *Dialectology Meets Typology: Dialect Grammar from a Cross Linguistic Perspective,* ed. B. Kortmann, 127–145. Berlin: Mouton De Gruyter.

Chaudenson, R. 1979. *Les creoles français.* Evreux: Nathan.

———. 1992. *Des îles, des hommes, des langues.* Paris: L'Harmattan.

———. 2001. *Creolization of Language and Culture.* London: Routledge.

Chierchia, G. 1998. Reference to kinds across languages. *Natural Language Semantics* 6: 339–405.

Chomsky, N. 1957. Syntactic Structures. The Hague: Mouton.

———. 1962. Discussion. In *Third Texas Conference on Problems of Linguistic Analysis in English,* ed. A. Hill, 124–169. Austin: University of Texas Press.

———. 1965. *Aspects of the Theory of Syntax.* Cambridge, MA: MIT Press.

———. 1970. Remarks on nominalization. In *Readings in English Transformational Grammar,* eds. R. Jacobs & P. Rosenbaum, 184–221. The Hague: Mouton.

———. 1981. *Lectures on Government and Binding.* Dordrecht: Foris.

———. 1986. *Knowledge of Language: Its Nature, Origin and Use.* New York: Praeger.

———. 1995. *The Minimalist Program.* Cambridge, MA: MIT Press.

———. 2000. Minimalist inquiries: The framework. In *Step by Step: Essays on Minimalist Syntax in Honor of Howard Lasnik,* eds. R. Martin et al., 89–155. Cambridge, MA: MIT Press.

———. 2001. Derivation by phase. In *Ken Hale: A Life in Linguistics,* ed. M. Kenstowicz, 1–52. Cambridge, MA: MIT Press.

———. 2002. Beyond explanatory adequacy. MIT *Occasional Papers in Linguistics,* no. 20, Department of Linguistics and Philosophy, MIT.

———. 2006. *Language and Mind.* 3rd ed. Cambridge, MA: MIT Press.

Chomsky, N., & H. Lasnik. 1993. Principles and parameters theory. In *Syntax: An International Handbook of Contemporary Research,* eds. A. Von Stechow, W. Sternefeld, 506–569. Berlin: de Gruyter.

Cinque, G. 1990. Ergative adjectives and the lexicalist hypothesis. *Natural Language and Linguistic Theory* 8: 1–40.

———. 1993. On the evidence for partial N-movement in the Romance DP. *Venice Working Papers in Linguistics* 3(2): 21–40.

———. 1994. On the evidence for partial N movement in the Romance DP. In *Paths towards Universal Grammar*, eds. G. Cinque, J. Koster, J.-Y. Pollock, L. Rizzi, & R. Zanuttini, 85–110. Washington, DC: Georgetown University Press.

———. 2004. Issues in adverbial syntax. *Lingua*, 114: 683–710.

———. 2005. Deriving Greenberg's universal 20 and its exceptions. *Linguistic Inquiry* 36: 315–332.

———. 2007. The fundamental left-right asymmetry of natural languages. *University of Venice Working Papers in Linguistics* 17: 77–107.

Clahsen, H., & P. Muysken. 1986. The availability of Universal Grammar to adult and child learners—a study of the acquisition of German word order. *Second Language Research* 2: 93–119.

Contreras, H. 1986. Spanish bare NPs and the ECP. In *Generative Studies in Spanish Syntax*, eds. I. Bordelois, H. Contreras, & K. Zagona, 25–49. Dordrecht: Foris.

Cornips, L. 2006. Variationist sociolinguistics—syntax. *Meertens Institute*, 2–12.

Cornips, L., & K. P. Corrigan. 2005. Toward an integrated approach to syntactic variation: A retrospective and prospective synopsis. In *Syntax and Variation: Reconciling the Biological and the Social*, eds. L. Cornips & K. P. Corrigan, 1–27. Amsterdam: Benjamins.

Cornips, L., & C. Poletto. 2005. On standardising syntactic elicitation techniques, part 1. *Lingua* 115: 939–957.

Crespo, A. 1995. *Esclavos negros en Bolivia*. La Paz: Librería Editorial Juventud.

Crisma, P. 1990. *Functional categories inside the NP: A study on the distribution of nominal modifiers*. PhD diss., University of Venice.

———. 1993. On adjective placement in Romance and Germanic event nouns. *Rivista di Grammatical Generativa* 18: 61–100.

Dalence, J. M. 1975. *Bosquejo estadístico de Bolivia: Bolivia en su historia*. La Paz: Editorial Universitaria.

DeCamp, D. 1971. Towards a generative analysis of a post-creole continuum. In *Pidginization and Creolization of Languages*, ed. D. Hymes, 349–370. Cambridge: Cambridge University Press.

DeGraff, M. 2003. Against creole exceptionalism. *Language* 79: 391–410.

———. 2004. Against creole exceptionalism redux*. *Language* 80: 834–839.

———. 2005. Linguists' most dangerous myth: The fallacy of Creolist exceptionalism. *Language in Society* 34: 533–591.

Delicado-Cantero, M., & S. Sessarego. 2011. Variation and syntax in number expression in Afro-Bolivian Spanish. In *Proceedings of the 13th Hispanic Linguistic Symposium*, ed. L. Ortiz-López, 42–53. Somerville, MA: Cascadilla Press.

Demonte, V. 2008. Meaning-form correlations and adjective position in Spanish. In *The semantics of adjectives and adverbs*. eds. C. Kennedy and L. Mc Nally. 71–100. Oxford University Press

den Dikken, M. 2003. *The Structure of the Noun Phrase in Rotuman*. Lincom Studies in Austronesian Linguistics 05, Munich: LINCOM Europa.

Depiante M., & P. Masullo. 2001. Género y número en la elipsis nominal: Consecuencia para la hipótesis lexicalista. Paper presented at *I Encuentro de gramática generativa*, Gral Roca, 22–24 November 2001.

Déprez, V. 2001. On the syntactic and semantic nature of Haitian bare NPs. In *Current Issues in Romance Linguistics: Selected Papers from the 29th Linguistics Symposium on Romance Languages*, eds. D. Cresti, C. Tortora, & T. Saterfield, 48–61. Amsterdam: John Benjamins.

Díaz-Campos, M., & C. Clements. 2005. Mainland Spanish colonies and Creole genesis: The Afro-Venezuelan area revisited. In *Proceedings of the Second Workshop on Spanish Sociolinguistics*, eds. S. Lotfi & M. Westmoreland, 41–53. Somerville, MA: Cascadilla Press.

———. 2008. A Creole origin for Barlovento Spanish? A linguistic and sociohistorical inquiry. *Language in Society* 37: 351–383.

Dowty, D. 1991. Thematic proto-roles and argument selection. *Language* 67(3): 547–619.

Epstein, S., S. Flynn, & G. Martohardjono. 1996. Second language acquisition: Theoretical and experimental issues in contemporary research. *Behavioral and Brain Sciences* 19: 677–714.

Frampton, J., & S. Gutmann. 2000. Agreement is feature sharing. http://www.math.neu.edu/ling/pdffiles/agrisfs.pdf.

Franceschina, F. 2002. Case and φ-feature agreement in advanced L2 Spanish grammars. In EUROSLA Yearbook, eds. S. Foster-Cohen, T. Ruthenberg, & M. L. Poschen, 71–86. Amsterdam: John Benjamins.

———. 2005. *Fossilized Second Language Grammars*. Amsterdam: John Benjamins.

Giorgi, A., & G. Longobardi. 1991. *The Syntax of Noun Phrases*. Cambridge: Cambridge University Press.

Goodman, M. 1987. The Portuguese element in the American creoles. In *Pidgin and Creole Languages: Essays in Memory of John E. Reinecke*, ed. G. G. Gilbert, 361–405. Honolulu: University of Hawaii Press.

Granda, G. de. 1978. *Estudios linguisticos hispanicos, afrohispanicos y criollos*. Madrid: Editorial Gredos.

Greenberg, Y. 2003. *Manifestations of Genericity*. New York: Routledge.

Grimshaw, J. 1990. *Argument Structure*. Cambridge, MA: MIT Press.

———. 1997. Projection, heads, and optimality. *Linguistic Inquiry* 28: 373–422.

Grohmann, K. K., & L. Haegeman. 2002. Resuming reflexives. In *Nordlyd* 31: 46–62.

Guéron, J. 1981. Logical operators, complete constituents, and extraction transformations. In *Levels of Syntactic Representation*, eds. R. May & J. Koster, 65–142. Dordrecht: Foris.

Gutiérrez-Rexach, J. 2004. *La semántica de los indefinidos*. Madrid: Arco Libros.

———. 2006. Beyond the indefiniteness restriction. *Sinn und Bedeutung* ed. E. Puig-Waldmüller, 291–304. Barcelona: Universitat Pompeu Fabra

Gutiérrez-Rexach, J., & E. Mallén. 2001. NP movement and adjective position in the DP phases. In *Features and Interfaces in Romance: Essays in Honor of Heles Contreras*, eds. J. Herschenshon, E. Mallén, & K. Zagona, 107–132. Amsterdam: John Benjamins.

Gutiérrez-Rexach, J., & S. Sessarego. 2011. Nominal reference and dialect variation in Spanish. In *Res per nomen: La référence, la conscience et le sujet énonciateur*, ed. P. Frath, 129–136. Reims: EPURE.

Gutiérrez-Rodríguez, E. 2009. Rasgos gramaticales de los cuantificadores débiles. PhD diss., Universidad Computense de Madrid.

Guy, G. 1981. *Linguistic variation in Brazilian Portuguese: Aspects of the phonology, syntax, and language history*. PhD diss., University of Pennsylvania.

———. 2004. Muitas linguas: The linguistic impact of Africans in colonial Brazil. In *Enslaving Connections: Changing Cultures of Africa and Brazil during the Era of Slavery*, eds. J. C. Curto & P. E. Lovejoy, 125–137. New York: Humanity Books.

Hale, K., & S. J. Keyser. 1993. On argument structure and the lexical expression of grammatical relations. In *The View from Building 20: Essays in Honor of Sylvain Bromberger*, eds. K. Hale & S. J. Keyser, 53–110. Cambridge, MA: MIT Press.

Harley, H., & E. Ritter. 2002. Person and number in pronouns: A feature geometric analysis. *Language* 78: 482–526.

Harris, J. W. 1991. The exponence of gender in Spanish. *Linguistic Inquiry* 22(1): 27–62.

Hawkins, R. 1998. The inaccessibility of formal features of functional categories in second language acquisition. Paper presented at the *Pacific Second Language Research Forum*, Tokyo, March 1998.

Heap, D. 2001. Split subject pronoun paradigms: Feature geometry and underspecification. In *Current Issues in Linguistic Theory: Selected Papers from the XXIXth Linguistic Symposium on Romance Languages*, eds. T. Satterfield, C. Tortora, & D. Crest, 124–139. Amsterdam: John Benjamins.

Henry, A. 2005. Idiolectal variation and syntactic theory. In *Syntax and Variation: Reconciling the Biological and the Social*, eds. L. Cornips & K. P. Corrigan, 109–122. Amsterdam: John Benjamins.

Herschensohn, J. 2000. *The Second Time Around: Minimalism and L2 Acquisition*. Amsterdam: Benjamins.

Higginbotham, J. 1985. On semantics. *Linguistic Inquiry* 16: 547–593.

Holm, J. 1992. Popular Brazilian Portuguese: A semi-creole. In *Actas do colóquio sobre crioulos de base lexical portuguesa*, eds. E. d'Andrade & A. Kihm, 37–66. Lisbon: Colibrí.

———. 2004. *Languages in Contact: The Partial Restructuring of Vernaculars*. Cambridge: Cambridge University Press.

Ishane, T. 2008. *The Layered DP: Form and Meaning of French Indefinites*. Linguistik Aktuell / Linguistics Today, vol. 124. Amsterdam: John Benjamins.

Jackendoff, R. 1990. *Semantic Structures*. Cambridge, MA: MIT Press.

Jacobs, B. 2008. Papiamentu: A diachronic analysis of its core morphology. *Phrasis* 2: 59–82.

———. 2009a. The origins of Old Portuguese features in Papiamentu. In *Leeward Voices: Fresh Perspectives on Papiamentu and the Literatures and Cultures of the ABC Islands*, eds. N. Faraclas, R. Severing, C. Weijer, & L. Echteld, 1: 11–38. Curaçao: FPI/ UNA.

———. 2009b. The Upper Guinea origins of Papiamentu: Linguistic and historical evidence. *Diachronica* 26(3): 319 379.

Kayne, R. 1994. *The Antisymmetry of Syntax*. Cambridge, MA: MIT Press.

———. 1996. Microparametric syntax: Some introductory remarks. In *Microparametric Syntax and Dialect Variation*, eds. J. R. Black & V. Motapanyane, ix–xxviii. Amsterdam: John Benjamins.

———. 2000. *Parameters and Universals*. Oxford: Oxford University Press.

Kempen, G., & E. Hoenkamp. 1987. An incremental procedural grammar for sentence formulation. *Cognitive Science* 11: 201–258.

Kester, E.-P., & C. Schmitt. 2007. Papiamentu and Brazilian Portuguese: A comparative study of bare nouns. In *Noun Phrases in Creole Languages*, eds. M. Baptista & J. Guéron, 107–144. Amsterdam: John Benjamins.

Kester, E.-P., & P. Sleeman. 2002. N-ellipsis in Spanish. In *Linguistics in the Netherlands 2002*, 107–116. Amsterdam: John Benjamins.

King, R., & T. Nadasdi. 1997. Left dislocation number marking and non-standard French. *Probus* 9: 267–284.

Klein, H. 1986. *African Slavery in Latin America and the Caribbean.* Oxford: Oxford University Press.

———. 1999. *A Concise History of Bolivia.* Cambridge: Cambridge University Press.

Koopman, H. 1997. The spec head configuration. In *Syntax at Sunset,* eds. E. Garrett & F. Lee, 37–65. UCLA Working Papers in Syntax and Semantics 1. Los Angeles: UCLA Department of Linguistics.

Kroch, A. 1989. Function and grammar in the history of English: Periphrastic "do." In *Language Change and Variation,* eds. R. Fasold & D. Schiffrin, 133–172. Amsterdam: Benjamins.

———. 1994. Morphosyntactic variation. http://www.sfb441.uni-tuebingen.de/veranstaltungen/morphosyntax.pdf.

Labov, W. 1966. *The social stratification of English in New York City.* Washington, DC: Center for Applied Linguistics.

———. 1969. Contraction, deletion and inherent variability of the English copula. *Language* 45: 715–762.

———. 1972. *Language in the Inner City.* Philadelphia: University of Pennsylvania Press.

———. 1984. Field methods of the project on linguistic change and variation. In *Language in Use,* eds. J. Baugh and J. Sherzer, 84–112. Englewood Cliffs, NJ: Prentice Hall.

Larson, B. 1998. *Cochabamba, 1550–1900.* Durham, NC: Duke University Press.

Larson, R. 1988. On the double object construction. *Linguistic Inquiry* 19(3): 335–391.

Laurence, K. 1974. Is Caribbean Spanish a case of decreolization? *Orbis* 23: 484–499.

Leonetti, M. 1990. *El artículo y la referencia.* Madrid: Taurus Universitaria.

Leonini, C. 2006. *The acquisition of object clitics and definite articles: Evidence from Italian as L2 and L1.* PhD diss., University of Florence.

Leons, W. 1984. Some notes on the demographic history of the Negro in the Bolivian Yungas. In *Anthropological Investigation in Bolivia,* eds. W. Leons & A. MacLean Spearman, 13–27. Museum of Anthropology, Miscellaneous Series 58. Greeley, CO: University of Northern Colorado, Museum of Anthropology.

Levelt, W. J. M. 1989. *Speaking: From Intention to Articulation.* Cambridge, MA: MIT Press.

Lipski, J. M. 1985. *The Spanish of Equatorial Guinea.* Tübingen: Max Niemeyer.

———. 1987. The Chota Valley: Afro-Hispanic Language in Highland, Ecuador. *Latin American Research Review* 22(1): 155–170.

———. 1992. El Valle del Chota: Enclave lingüístico afroecuatoriano. *Boletín de la Academia Puertorriqueña de la Lengua Española* 10: 21–36.

———. 1993. *On the Non-Creole Basis for Afro-Caribbean Spanish.* Albuquerque: University of New Mexico Press.

———. 1994. *Latin American Spanish.* New York: Longman.

———. 1998. El español bozal. In *América negra: Panorámica actual de los estudios lingüísticos sobre variedades criollas y afrohispanas,* eds. M. Perl & A. Schwegler, 293–327. Frankfurt: Vervuert.

———. 2000. Bozal Spanish: Restructuring or creolization? In *Degrees of Restructuring in Creole Languages,* ed. Edgar W. Schneider & Ingrid Neuman-Holzschuh, 55–83. Amsterdam: John Benjamins.

———. 2005. *A History of Afro-Hispanic Language: Five Centuries, Five Continents.* Cambridge: Cambridge University Press.

———. 2006a. Afro-Bolivian Spanish and Helvetia Portuguese: Semi-creole parallels. *Papia* 16: 96–116.

——. 2006b. Morphosyntactic implications in Afro-Hispanic language: New data on creole pathways. *Paper presented at the 35th New Ways of Analyzing Variation Conference,* Columbus: The Ohio State University, October 2006. http://www.personal.psu.edu/ jm134/ afmorph.pdf.

——. 2007. Afro-Bolivian Spanish: The survival of a true creole prototype. In *Synchronic and Diachronic Perspectives on Contact Languages,* eds. M. Huber & V. Velupillai, 175–198. Creole Language Library 32. Amsterdam: John Benjamins.

——. 2008. *Afro-Bolivian Spanish.* Madrid: Iberoamericana—Vervuert.

——. 2009. Afro-Choteño speech: Towards the recreation of "Black Spanish." *Negritud* 2: 99–120.

——. 2011a. Decreolization as emergent grammars: Some Afro-Bolivian data. *Journal of Pidgin and Creole Languages* 26: 276–340.

——. 2011b. El "nuevo" Palenquero y el español afroboliviano: ¿Es reversible la descriollización? In *Selected Proceedings of the 13th Hispanic Linguistics Symposium,* ed. L. Ortiz-López, 1–16. Somerville, MA: Cascadilla Press.

——. n. d. Spanish-based creoles in the Caribbean. Unpublished manuscript. http://www. personal.psu.edu/jm134/spcreole.pdf.

Lobeck, A. 1995. *Ellipsis: Functional Heads, Licensing and Identification.* New York: Oxford University Press.

Lockhart, J. 1994. *Spanish Peru, 1532–1560: A Social History.* Madison: University of Wisconsin Press.

Longobardi, G. 1994. Reference and proper names: A theory of N-movement in syntax and logical form. *Linguistic Inquiry* 25: 609–665.

Macera, P. 1966. *Instrucciones para el Manejo de las Haciendas Jesuítas del Perú, ss. XVII–XVIII.* Lima: Universidad Nacional Mayor de San Marcos.

Martinus, F. 1989. West African connection: The influence of the Afro-Portuguese on the Papiamentu of Curazao. In *Estudios sobre español de América y lingüística afroamericana,* 288–289. Bogota: Publicaciones del Instituto Caro y Cuervo.

McNally, L. 2004. Bare plurals in Spanish are interpreted as properties. *Catalan Journal of Linguistics* 3: 115–133.

McWhorter, J. 1997. *Towards a New Model of Creole Genesis.* New York: Peter Lang.

——. 1998. Identifying the creole prototype: Vindicating a typological class. *Language* 74: 788–818.

——. 2000. *The Missing Spanish Creole.* Berkeley: University of California Press.

——. 2001. The world's simplest grammars are creole grammars. Special issue, *Linguistic Typology* 5(2/3): 125–166.

Megenney, W. 1985. África en Venezuela: Su herencia lingüística y cultura literaria. *Montalbán* 15: 3–56.

Mellafe, R. 1984. *La introducción de la esclavitud negra en Chile: Tráfico y rutas.* Santiago: Editorial Universitaria.

Merchant, J. 2001. *The Syntax of Silence.* Oxford: Oxford University Press.

Mintz, S. 1971. The socio-historical background to pidginization and creolization. In *Pidginization and Creolization of Languages,* ed. D. Hymes, 481–498. Cambridge: Cambridge University Press.

Mufwene, S. 1996. The founder principle in creole genesis. *Diachronica* 13: 83–134.

———. 1997. Jargons, pidgins creoles and koines: What are they? In *The Structure and Status of Pidgins and Creoles*, eds. Arthur Spears & Donald Winford, 35-70. Amsterdam: John Benjamins.

Müller, A. 2003. Generic sentences with indefinite and bare subjects in Brazilian Portuguese. In *Proceedings of SULA 2*, eds. J. Anderssen, P. Menéndez-Benito, & A. Werle, 71-86. Vancouver: Amherst: GLSA.

Munn, A., & C. Schmitt. 2001. Bare nominals and the morphosyntax of number. In *Current Issues in Romance Linguistics*, eds. T. Satterfield, C. Tortora, & D. Cresti, 217-231. Amsterdam: John Benjamins.

Muysken, P., & N. Smith. 2005. The study of pidgin and creole languages. In *Pidgins and Creoles: An Introduction*, eds. J. Arends, P. Muysken, & N. Smith, 3-14. Amsterdam: John Benjamins.

Naro, A., & M. M. Scherre. 2000. Variable concord in Portuguese: The situation in Brazil and Portugal. In *Language Change and Language Contact in Pidgins and Creoles*, ed. J. McWhorter, 235-255. Amsterdam: John Benjamins.

Nowak, M. 2002. Computational and evolutionary aspects of language. *Nature* 417: 611-617.

Nowak, M., N. Komarova, & P. Niyogi. 2001. Evolution of Universal Grammar. *Science* 291: 114-118.

Parrott, J. 2007. Distributed morphological mechanisms of Labovian variation in morphosyntax. PhD diss., Georgetown University.

Partee, B., & M. Rooth. 1983. Generalized conjunction and type ambiguity. In *Meaning, Use and Interpretation of Language*, eds. R. Bäuerle, C. Schwarze, & A. von Stechow, 361-383. Berlin: Walter de Gruyter.

Pérez Inofuentes, D. M. 2010. *Las huellas lingüísticas de África en Bolivia: El habla afroyungueña*. Master's thesis, University of Zurich.

Pesetsky, D., & E. Torrego. 2007. The syntax of valuation and the interpretability of features. In *Phrasal and Clausal Architecture: Syntactic Derivation and Interpretation*, eds. S. Karimi, V. Samiian, & W. K. Wilkins, 262-294. Amsterdam: Benjamins.

Picallo, C. 1991. Nominals and nominalizations in Catalan. *Probus* 3: 279-316.

———. 2008. Gender and number in romance. *Lingue e Linguaggio* 1: 47-66.

———. 2010. Structure of the noun phrase. In *Handbook of Hispanic Linguistics*, eds. A. Olarrea, E. O'Rourke, J. I. Hualde, 263-285. Oxford: Blackwell.

Pienemann, M. 1998. *Language Processing and Second Language Development: Processability Theory*. Amsterdam: John Benjamins.

———. 2000. Psycholinguistic mechanisms in the development of English as a second language. In *Language Use, Language Acquisition and Language History: Mostly Empirical Studies in Honour of Rudiger Zimmermann*, eds. I. Plag & K. P. Schneider, 99-118. Trier: Wissenschaftlicher Verlag Trier.

———, ed. 2005. *Cross-linguistic Aspects of Processability Theory*. Amsterdam: John Benjamins.

Pizarroso Cuenca, A. 1977. *La cultura negra en Bolivia*. La Paz: Instituto Boliviano de Cultura.

Plag, I. 2008a. Creoles as interlanguages: Inflectional morphology. *Journal of Pidgin and Creole Languages* 23(1): 109-130.

———. 2008b. Creoles as interlanguages: Syntactic structures. *Journal of Pidgin and Creole Languages* 23(2): 307-328.

———. 2009a. Creoles as interlanguages: Phonology. *Journal of Pidgin and Creole Languages* 24(1): 119-138.

―――. 2009b. Creoles as interlanguages: Word-formation. *Journal of Pidgin and Creole Languages* 24(2): 339–362.

Poletto, C. 2000. *The Higher Functional Field: Evidence from Northern Italian Dialects*. Oxford: Oxford University Press.

Pollard, C., & I. A. Sag. 1994. *Head-Driven Phrase Structure Grammar*. Chicago: University of Chicago Press.

Pollock, J.-Y. 1989. Verb movement, Universal Grammar and the structure of IP. *Linguistic Inquiry* 20: 365–424.

Pomino N., & E. Stark. 2009. Adnominal adjectives in romance: Where morphology seemingly meets semantics. In *Proceedings of the IV Nereus International Workshop "Definiteness and DP Structure in Romance Languages,"* eds. M. T. Espinal, M. Leonetti, & L. McNally, 113–135. Konstanz: Arbeitspapiere des Fachbereichs Sprachwissenschaft.

Poplack, S. 1979. Function and process in a variable phonology. PhD diss., University of Pennsylvania.

―――. 1980. Deletion and disambiguation in Puerto Rican Spanish. *Language* 56(2): 371–385.

Portugal Ortiz, M. 1977. *La esclavitud negra en las épocas colonial y nacional de Bolivia*. La Paz: Instituto Boliviano de Cultura.

Prince, A., & P. Smolensky. 1993/2004. *Optimality Theory: Constraint Interaction in Generative Grammar*. Oxford: Blackwell.

Raposo, E. 1999. Towards a minimalist account of nominal anaphora in Spanish and English. http://www.ling.umd.edu/courses/Ling819/Papers/edu.html.

Ritter, E. 1991. Two functional categories in noun phrases: Evidence from Modern Hebrew. In *Perspectives on Phrase Structure: Heads and Licensing*, ed. S. Rothstein, 37–62. Syntax and Semantics 25. San Diego: Academic Press.

―――. 1993. Where is gender? *Linguistic Inquiry* 24: 795–803.

Roberts, C. 2001. Demonstratives as definites. In *Information Sharing: Reference and Presupposition in Language Generation and Interpretation,* eds. Kees van Deemter & Roger Kibble, 89–196. Stanford, CA: CSLI.

―――. 2003. Uniqueness in definite noun phrases. *Linguistics & Philosophy* 26: 287–350.

Romaine, S. 1988. *Pidgin and Creole Languages*. London: Longman.

Rosemblat, Á. 1954. *La poblacion indigena y el mestizaje en America*. Buenos Aires: Editorial NOVA

Saab, A. 2004. *El dominio de la elipsis nominal en español: Identidad estricta e inserción tardía*. Master's thesis, Universidad Nacional del Comahue.

Sánchez, L., & M. Giménez. 1998. The L2 acquisition of definite determiners: From null to overt. In *Proceedings of the 22nd Annual Boston University Conference on Language Development,* 640–650. Somerville, MA: Cascadilla.

Sankoff, G., S. Tagliamonte, & E. Smith. 2005. Goldvarb X: A variable rule application for Macintosh and Windows. Department of Linguistics, University of Toronto. http://individual.utoronto.ca/tagliamonte/goldvarb.htm

Scherre, M. 2001. Phrase-level parallelism effect on noun phrase number agreement. *Language Variation and Change* 13: 91–107.

Schmitt, C., & A. Munn. 2003. The syntax and semantics of bare arguments Brazilian Portuguese. *Linguistic Variation Yearbook* 2: 185–216.

Schneider, E. 1990. English World-Wide: The cline of creoleness in English-oriented creoles and semi-creoles of the Caribbean. *English World-Wide* 11: 79–113.

Schwartz, B. 1996. Now for some facts, with a focus on development and an explicit role for L1. *Behavioral and Brain Sciences* 19: 739–40.

———. 1998. The second language instinct. *Lingua* 106: 133–160.

Schwartz, B., & R. Sprouse. 1996. L2 cognitive states and the full transfer/full access model. *Second Language Research* 12: 40–72.

Schwegler, A. 1991. Negation in Palenquero. *Journal of Pidgin and Creole Languages* 6(2): 165–214.

———. 1993. Rasgos afro-portugueses en el criollo del Palenque de San Basilio Colombia. In *Homenaje a José Pérez Vidal*, ed. C. Díaz Alayón, 667–696. La Laguna, Tenerife: Litografia A. Romero.

———. 1996. La doble negación dominicana y la génesis del español caribeño. *Hispanic Linguistics* 8: 247–315.

———. 1999. Monogenesis revisited: The Spanish perspective. In *Creole Genesis, Attitudes and Discourse*, eds. J. Rickford & S. Romaine, 235–262. Amsterdam: John Benjamins.

———. 2007. Bare nouns in Palenquero: A fresh consensus in the making. In *Noun Phrases in Creole Languages: A Multi-Faceted Approach*, eds. M. Baptista & J. Guéron, 205–222. Amsterdam: John Benjamins.

———. 2010. Pidgin and creole studies: Their interface with Hispanic and Lusophone linguistics. *Studies in Hispanic and Lusophone Linguistics* 3(2): 431–481.

Schwegler, A., & T. Morton. 2003. Vernacular Spanish in a microcosm: *Kateyano* in El Palenque de San Basilio Colombia. *Revista Internacional de Lingüística Iberoamericana* 1: 97–159.

Schwenter, S. 2005. The pragmatics of negation in Brazilian Portuguese. *Lingua* 115: 1427–1456.

Sessarego, S. 2009. On the evolution of Afro-Bolivian Spanish subject-verb agreement: Variation and change. *Sintagma* 21: 107–119.

———. 2011. *Introducción al idioma afroboliviano: Una conversación con el awicho Manuel Barra.* Cochabamba: Plural Editores.

———. 2013. *Chota Valley Spanish.* Madrid: Iberoamericana—Vervuert.

———. n. d. Afro-Peruvian Spanish: Shedding light on the evolution of a missing Spanish creole.

Sessarego, S., & J. Gutiérrez-Rexach. 2011. A minimalist account for gender agreement in the Afro-Bolivian determiner phrase. *Folia Linguistica* 45(2): 465–488.

———. 2012. Variation, universals, and contact-induced change: Language evolution across generations and domains. In *Current Formal Aspects of Spanish Syntax and Semantics*, eds. M. González-Rivera & S. Sessarego, 251–270. Newcastle: Cambridge Scholars Publishing.

Seuren, P., & H. Wekker. 1986. Semantic transparency as a factor in Creole genesis. In *Substrata versus Universals in Creole Genesis*, eds. P. Muysken & N. Smith, 57–70. Amsterdam: Benjamins.

Simioni, L. 2007. A concordância de número no DP: Propostas minimalistas. *Estudos Lingüísticos* 36(1): 117–125.

Singler, J. 1992. Nativization and pidgin/creole genesis: A reply to Bickerton. *Journal of Pidgin and Creole Languages* 7: 319–333.

Slabakova, R. 2009. What is easy and what is hard to acquire in a second language? In *Proceedings of the 10th Generative Approaches to Second Language Acquisition Conference (GASLA 2009)*, eds. Melissa Bowles et al., 280–294. Somerville, MA: Cascadilla Proceedings Project.

Soux, M. L. 1993. Esclavos, peones y mingas: Apuntes sobre la fuerza de trabajo en las haciendas Yungueñas a principios de la república. *Historia y Cultura* 21: 51–58.

Speas, M. 1990. *Phrase Structure in Natural Language.* Dordrecht: Kluwer.

Sportiche, D. 1990. Movement, agreement and case. http://www.linguistics.ucla.edu/people/sportich/papers/mac.pdf.

Szabolcsi, A. 1983. The possessor that ran away from home. *Linguistic Review* 3: 89–102.

———. 1987. Functional categories in the noun phrase. In *Approaches to Hunfarian* (vol 2). ed. I. Kenesei, 167–189. Szaged: JATE.

———. 1989. Noun phrases and clauses: Is DP analogous to IP or CP? Unpublished manuscript. https://files.nyu.edu/as109/public/szabolcsi%20DP%20IP%20CP.pdf.

———. 1994. The noun phrase. In *The Syntactic Structure of Hungarian,* eds. F. Kiefer & K. E. Kiss, 179–274. Syntax and Semantics 27. San Diego: Academic Press.

Tagliamonte, S. 2006. *Analysing Sociolinguistic Variation.* Cambridge: Cambridge University Press.

Tesar, B., & P. Smolensky. 1998. Learnability in optimality theory. *Linguistic Inquiry* 29: 229–268.

Thomason, S., & T. Kaufman. 1988. *Language Contact, Creolization and Genetic Linguistics.* Berkeley: University of California Press.

Ticio, M. E. 2003. *On the structure of DPs.* PhD diss., University of Connecticut, Storrs.

———. 2005. NP-ellipsis in Spanish. *Proceedings of the 7th Hispanic Linguistics Symposium* 7: 128–141.

Torrego, E. 1988. Evidence for Determiner Phrases, Unpublished manuscript. University of Massachusetts, Boston.

Travis, L. 1984. Parameters and effects of word order variation. PhD diss., MIT.

Valois, D. 1991. The internal structure of DP. PhD diss., UCLA.

van Craenenbroeck, J. 2010. *The Syntax of Ellipsis: Evidence from Dutch Dialects.* Oxford: Oxford University Press.

van Gelderen, E. 2005. Principles and parameters in change. In *Syntax and Variation: Reconciling the Biological and the Social,* eds. L. Cornips & K. P. Corrigan, 179–198. Amsterdam: John Benjamins.

Wasow, T. 2002. *Postverbal Behavior.* Stanford, CA: CSLI.

Watson, A. 1989. *Slave Law in the Americas.* Athens, GA: University of Georgia Press.

Weinrich U., W. Labov, & M. Herzog. 1968. Empirical foundations for a theory of language change. In *Directions for Historical Linguistics,* eds. W. P. Lehmann & Y. Malkiel, 95–188. Austin: University of Texas Press.

Weiß, H. 2001. On two types of natural languages: Some consequences for linguistics. *Theoretical Linguistics* 27: 87–103.

Winford, D. 2000. "Intermediate" creoles and degrees of change in creole formation: The case of Bajan. In *Degrees of Restructuring in Creole Languages,* eds. I. Neumann-Holzschuh & E. Schneider, 215–246. Creole Language Library 22. Amsterdam: John Benjamins:

Wolff, I. 1981. Esclavitud y tráfico de negros en el Alto Perú, 1545–1640. *Historia y Cultura* 4: 37–63.

Zamparelli, R. 2000. *Layers in the Determiner Phrase.* New York: Garland.

Index

Note: Page numbers with *n* refer to footnotes. Throughout the index, *ABS* refers to Afro-Bolivian Spanish.

THEORETICAL DEVELOPMENTS IN HISPANIC LINGUISTICS
Javier Gutiérrez-Rexach, Series Editor

This book series aims to be an outlet for monographs or edited volumes addressing current problems and debates within Hispanic linguistics. The series will be open to a wide variety of areas and approaches, as long as they are grounded in theoretical goals and methodologies. Contributions from the disciplines of syntax, semantics, pragmatics, morphology, phonology, phonetics, etc. are welcome, as well as those analyzing interface issues or the historical development, acquisition, processing, and computation of grammatical properties. Research topics of interest are those dealing with Spanish or other Hispanic languages, in any of their dialects and varieties.

The Afro-Bolivian Spanish Determiner Phrase: A Microparametric Account
  SANDRO SESSAREGO

Interfaces and Domains of Quantification
  JAVIER GUTIÉRREZ-REXACH

CPSIA information can be obtained
at www.ICGtesting.com
Printed in the USA
FFOW04n0227220316
22496FF